Interpreting Our Heritage

Interpreting
Our Heritage

FREEMAN TILDEN

Fourth Edition, Expanded and Updated

Edited by R. BRUCE CRAIG

Foreword by RUSSELL E. DICKENSON

THE UNIVERSITY OF NORTH CAROLINA PRESS   Chapel Hill

© 2007 The University of North Carolina Press
Chapters 1–15 previously published as *Interpreting Our Heritage*, by Freeman Tilden, © 1957, 1967, 1977
The University of North Carolina Press.
Chapters 16–20 previously published as indicated on the opening page of each chapter.
Set in Arnhem type by Tseng Information Systems, Inc.
Manufactured in the United States of America
The paper in this book meets the guidelines for permanence and durability of the Committee on Production Guidelines for Book Longevity of the Council on Library Resources.

Library of Congress Cataloging-in-Publication Data
Tilden, Freeman, 1883–1980.
Interpreting our heritage / Freeman Tilden ; edited by R. Bruce Craig ; foreword by Russell E. Dickenson. — 4th ed., expanded and updated
    p. cm.
Included bibliographical references and index.
ISBN 978-0-8078-3180-9 (cloth : alk. paper) —
ISBN 978-0-8078-5867-7 (pbk. : alk. paper)
1. National parks and reserves—Interpretive programs—United States. 2. Historic sites—Interpretive programs—United States. I. Craig, R. Bruce. II. Title.
SB482.A4T53 2008
363.6'80973—dc22   2007033026

cloth   11 10 09 08 07   5 4 3 2 1
paper   11 10 09 08 07   5 4 3 2 1

The National Parks Conservation Association and the Coalition of National Park Service Retirees generously supported the publication of this work.

CONTENTS

ILLUSTRATIONS

I was fortunate to begin my career with the National Park Service as a park ranger at the end of World War II. One of the finest park interpreters at that time was Dr. Harold C. Bryant, superintendent of Grand Canyon National Park from 1940 to 1954 and considered by many to be the father and prime mover of national park interpretation dating from the 1920s. Also at Grand Canyon was park naturalist Louis Shellbach, who excelled in explaining canyon geology and the ancient landscapes of the region at the famed Yavapai Observation Station. Visitors were enthralled and appreciative of these special interpreters for their erudition and dramatic presentations, as was I.

Of course, there were many other excellent naturalists and interpreters in the National Park Service. But expansion of the service, new personnel, retirement of key people, and new leadership in the 1950s and 1960s called for a review of the program.

Enter Freeman Tilden.

In 1957 Freeman Tilden's *Interpreting Our Heritage* was published, introducing his six fundamental principles that should drive all interpretive services. His ideas have had enormous influence. The clarity of his principles and the simplicity of understanding revealed in the book led to widespread appeal. It has become required reading for new and seasoned interpreters alike. Tilden urged fledgling interpreters to help park visitors find more than facts and information. He suggested that interpretation's function should implore visitors to better understand themselves and to find personal meaning and inspiration in park resources. These ideas underlie the training of interpreters today.

In later life, Tilden never lost touch with the parks. In the early 1970s he traveled over 30,000 miles with Walt Dabney, a young national park ranger, to provide further realistic guidance to the National Park Service on emerging environmental issues. During this extended trip, Tilden repeatedly told audiences that "we are not doing enough. . . . We are entering into a world of crisis . . . something needs to be added. The interpreter should have a wider knowledge of what is going on in the world." He felt that the National Park Service should be using interpretation to foster sound environmental morals. This counsel was true in 1972; it is equally true today.

In his association with parks, Tilden developed an interest in how the national parks shaped American identity as well as individual identity, urging citizens to derive meaning and inspiration for and from precious natural and historical resources. This collection of essays by Freeman Tilden, with an introduction by R. Bruce Craig, offers many insights into the thinking of Tilden.

As director of the National Park Service from 1980 to 1985 and throughout my forty-year career, I was a witness to the awesome power of great interpretation. Interpreters decide what stories to tell, how to tell them, and who to tell them to, a serious responsibility. These essays once again remind us of the importance of Tilden's contribution to parks, to the practice of interpretation, and to the users of parks and other protected areas. His recommendations and observations made in another era retain their relevance today.

I encourage you to read this fine collection of works by Freeman Tilden.

RUSSELL E. DICKENSON
Former Director of the National Park Service
Seattle, Washington
April 23, 2007

ACKNOWLEDGMENTS

Thanks to David Perry, editor-in-chief of the University of North Carolina Press, for his guidance, patience, and thoughtful suggestions. He is a joy to work with, as are his assistant Zach Read and editor Jay Mazzocchi. Thanks also to former director Russell Dickenson for penning the thoughtful new foreword, and to Emily Weisner, my research assistant at the National Coalition for History. It was Emily who gathered essays and research materials at the National Archives; and laurels and accolades to her also for first entering Tilden's words onto the computer. I am grateful to David Nathanson, librarian at the National Park Service's Harpers Ferry Center, for delving into the center's library in search of Tilden's more obscure works; to Susanne Pichler, librarian at the Andrew Mellon Foundation (which holds the papers of the Old Dominion Foundation), for her effort to locate Tilden's original manuscript of *Interpreting Our Heritage*; and to Michael Grimes and Joe Schwartz, National Archives and Records Administration archivists, who tracked down Tilden's few existing references, letters, and unpublished reports in Record Group 79. I also would like to thank the manuscript's readers and technical reviewers, including Candace Shea, a Tilden biographer, and Corky Mayo, the chief interpreter of the National Park Service; and the National Parks Conservation Association and Alfred A. Knopf publishers for permission to reprint Tilden's works from their books and publications.

In the realm of photography, a hearty thanks to Dan Riss—not only for finding the time to secure photographs of Freeman Tilden from the Harpers Ferry Interpretive Design Center, but also for taking a number of photographs needed to round out the edition that were not readily available from my personal collection or from the National Park Service Digital Archive. And a very special thanks to Lee and Dottie Belanger for granting permission to reproduce previously unpublished photographs of Tilden from family albums.

Last but certainly not least: this project would not have been possible without the financial support of the National Parks Conservation Association and the Coalition of National Park Service Retirees.

R. BRUCE CRAIG

Interpreting Our Heritage

Freeman Tilden (National Park Service photo by M. Woodbridge Williams)

For fifty years, interpreters at national, state, and municipal parks, nature reserves, museums, battlefields, and historic homes and sites have turned to Freeman Tilden's *Interpreting Our Heritage* to provide a philosophical underpinning for their art and craft. Since 1957 it has been *the* interpretive primer, a classic that has influenced interpretation more than any other single work. Even the most experienced interpreter reaches for it from time to time to reread and refresh his or her memory. And invariably, in each successive reading, new insights come to light that in previous readings escaped notice. Because of its timeless concepts, ideas, and underlying philosophy, it is the one book on professional heritage interpreters' bookshelves that rarely gathers dust.

My introduction to Tilden's work came in 1976, when, fresh out of college, I was hired by the National Park Service (NPS) to give guided tours of Philadelphia's Independence Hall and deliver talks to visitors who wanted to see and touch the Liberty Bell. Like many of the dozens of other young people who were hired in that bicentennial year, I thought I brought to the position a pretty good grasp of American history. After all, I had majored in the subject in college, and I also possessed a teaching credential. I felt confident that with my history degree and specialized graduate-level coursework in social studies pedagogy, I was well prepared to spend my summer "teaching" park visitors about the era of the American Revolution. Then, during the brief weeklong training given to all new park interpreters, I came to realize that much of my college education was rendered useless. The culprit: a book that we were required to read, Freeman Tilden's *Interpreting Our Heritage*.

Reading Tilden's book was our first assignment. After that, we were subjected to an intense interpretive training program that was unlike anything I had experienced in college. It was actually a crash course in communication, nuts and bolts training to the core. We learned that interpretation was a specialized form of education, but it was also something more—an activity perhaps best characterized as a unique form of communication. We learned how to choose topics, develop themes, and become good storytellers. But each day we kept coming back to Tilden's famous "six principles." We were assured that if we applied them to our talks and tours we would make fine interpreters.

Though we had been provided with a copy of the book, there was nothing in it to tell us who this man Freeman Tilden was—not even a biographical note in the back of the book. Nothing. We were merely told by our instructors that he was something akin to an NPS "guru," a thoughtful, insightful, inspired man who on occasion gave moving and informative talks to young rangers at the NPS Stephen T. Mather Training Center in Harpers Ferry, West Virginia. And of course, he wrote this important book that helped park rangers become skilled in the art and craft of interpretation. That, however, was about all we were told. I wanted to know more.

Unfortunately, there was a thirty-year hiatus between then and the time that I was actually able to devote the necessary energy to learning more about Tilden. Though I won the NPS's Freeman Tilden Award and immediately after that spent a number of years as a trainer at the Mather Training Center, I never had the good fortune of meeting Tilden personally. Tilden died in 1980, but even after he was gone, his presence at Mather was still felt. A little shrine was set up in his memory in the training center lounge, featuring his walking stick, his hat, and several other sacrosanct Tilden relics. Like the thousands of others who never met Tilden personally, I grew to know him through his writings.

A BRIEF TILDEN BIOGRAPHY

Freeman Tilden was born on August 22, 1883, in Malden, Massachusetts, north of Boston. He was the eighth of nine children. Like many sons and daughters of gentrified New Englanders, he was educated by private tutors. His father, Samuel Tilden, was a successful newspaperman, and he encouraged his son to write. At an early age, Freeman began contributing columns and book reviews to his father's paper, the *Boston Transcript*. Although his father expected him to attend Harvard University after his graduation from high school, Freeman instead chose to see the world. He traveled extensively, learned bits of various foreign languages (eventually becoming fluent in several), and returned home convinced that he wanted to become a foreign correspondent.

At age nineteen, following in his father's footsteps, Tilden joined the staff of the *Boston Globe* and began a career as a working journalist. In time he would also serve as a reporter for the *Boston Herald*, the *Charleston News and Courier*, and the *New York Evening Post*. At one point he moved to England, where he became European correspondent for the *Saturday Evening Post* and *Ladies' Home Journal*. By the end of his career, he had worked for nearly a dozen newspapers and magazines.

In October 1909, after returning from Europe and Buenos Aires (where he was employed briefly by the English newspaper the *Standard*), Tilden married Mabel S. Martin, a schoolteacher who lived in Ludlow, Vermont. After they were wed, the couple lived in New York City, but not for long. For years, Tilden and his growing family (ultimately he and Mabel would have four children) lived what one of his children recalled as a "nomadic life" in the United States and abroad, as Tilden searched for meaning and purpose in his writing and work. In time, he and his family settled in Warner, a small town in southern New Hampshire.

Tilden seemed well suited to the writer's life. He was well read, intelligent, and a keen observer of human nature. Not too long after launching his career in journalism, and like many other writers with a creative bent, he began writing fiction during his spare time. At first he wrote short stories and poems, then novels (the first being published in 1915), plays, and radio serials. All told he authored twenty-five books of fiction and nonfiction, and hundreds of his short stories and articles appeared in such popular magazines as *Country Gentleman*, *Collier's Weekly*, and the *Saturday Evening Post*, where he was a correspondent for ten years.

For some twenty-five years, Tilden's work was in high demand. Throughout his writing career, he spent a good deal of time in New York City and Washington, D.C., where he was a literary associate of H. L. Mencken, O. Henry, and other literary luminaries. In 1939 Tilden returned to New Hampshire and started to pen his own newsletter, *The Open Door*. Subscribers eagerly watched their mailboxes for the periodical, in which, for a mere dollar a year, readers enjoyed

Even as a working journalist and newspaper correspondent, Tilden appreciated the inspiration that came from working outdoors. (Photo courtesy of Lee and Dottie Belanger)

Tilden and his wife, Mabel, lived a nomadic life in the United States and abroad before settling down in New Hampshire. (Photo courtesy of Lee and Dottie Belanger)

Tilden's views on just about everything from politics to the collegiate fad of goldfish swallowing.

At fifty-eight, an age at which most people begin looking forward to retirement, Tilden abandoned fiction writing and embarked on a new phase of his career. This time he wanted to work in a writing medium that dealt only with, as he characterized it, "the facts."

The search for a new focus for his remarkable talents required thoughtful consideration. He assessed his relative strengths as a writer, gauged his interests, and evaluated various writing avenues that he thought would suit him. One day, at the Players Club in Manhattan, Tilden had a brief encounter with Newton Drury, the director of the National Park Service. At the private club, Drury enthralled Tilden with tales of Yosemite, Yellowstone, the Grand Canyon, and other national parks. Having long been a conservationist at heart, and having periodically written on conservation-related topics for years, Tilden became enchanted with the idea of the national parks. He concluded that he had found the creative focus he was looking for.

In the winter of 1941, Tilden confidently strode into Drury's office and sat down. He explained to the director that he was tired of writing fiction "merely to entertain," and that at this point in his career he wanted to turn his attention elsewhere, one of his goals being to write "something serious." He also told Drury that he had "become desirous of providing efforts that would be more significant to the world."

Drury recognized that Tilden possessed "a delicate sense of humor and a keen perception of human nature." And not wanting to lose the talented gift horse that sat in the chair in front of him, Drury knighted Tilden with the title "administrative assistant" and gave him carte blanche to roam the National Park System. His charge: to formulate a plan for public relations and interpretation.

Tilden quickly settled into his new niche. He began traveling the national parks and working on the task Drury assigned to him. But in December 1943, Tilden began to look beyond the national parks and started visiting state parks as well. So began the longed-for second career. Over the next four decades, thousands of words about the national and state parks flowed from Tilden's pen. And as he had hoped, his words were no longer written merely to entertain readers—though they certainly were entertaining—but to inform and educate them as well.

TILDEN'S WRITINGS ON NATIONAL PARKS

Tilden's first book on the parks emerged out of his initial series of travels. As it happened, a friend of Drury, New York publisher Alfred Knopf, had made a trip to the American West and developed an interest in conservation and the national parks. He wanted to publish a book about the nation's parks, and Drury—by now fully convinced of Tilden's insightful perspectives on the meaning of parks—suggested Tilden for the job.

In 1951 Knopf published Tilden's *The National Parks: What They Mean to You and Me*. The book was a milestone in nature and conservation publishing, completely unlike the travelogues and guidebooks then on bookstore shelves. *The National Parks* reflected Tilden's intensely personal views on parks and conservation. The first four chapters, for example, were devoted to explaining the philosophy of the national park "system" as envisioned and internalized by Tilden. One chapter from the revised edition of that book (1986), titled "That Elderly Schoolma'am: Nature"—the chapter that explains to a lay audience what interpretation is designed to bring to visitors' understanding of parks and the park experience—is just as relevant today as it was fifty years ago. Consequently, it is reproduced in this volume. Needless to say, Knopf was delighted with Tilden's manuscript and boasted that it would become "the best book ever written" on the national parks.

Tilden continued in his consultant role through the administrations of several park service directors. In 1953 NPS director Conrad Wirth enlisted Tilden's considerable talents to write a different type of book—different for the park service, at least, but one that Tilden, experienced in public relations, was ideally suited to draft. His assignment was to write a thoughtful, extended essay that could be put in the hands of potential major donors, the goal being to help convince them of the need to contribute money to the National Park Service. The book was timely, as Wirth had just launched the MISSION 66 initiative—a massive and costly scheme spearheaded by the director that he hoped would reinvigorate the NPS in time for its centennial in 1966.

In *The Fifth Essence* (published by the National Park Trust Fund Board), Tilden coined the term used for the title of the book, defining it as those actions that major donors could take to preserve significant places of beauty and "to keep living, accessible, and dynamic the steps of our history." The classy, slip-cased, limited-edition book is an example of Tilden's exceptional public-relations efforts. And, when put in the right hands, *The Fifth Essence* did help attract private-sector funds to help meet the goals of MISSION 66.

After completing the text for *The Fifth Essence*, Tilden spent some time "ruminating"—"as a cow chews cud," he recalled—and decided to focus his attention back on the subject that had first captivated his interest in the parks: interpretation. In a letter to Director Wirth written back in September 1952, Tilden had set the stage for this next project when he stated that while interpretation in the parks was "not bad," something critical was missing. That missing something, Tilden told Wirth, was an underlying "basic philosophy."

Wirth, however, already possessed a philosophy regarding the goal and mission of park interpretation. His notion encompassed an innovative if not radical idea for the mid-1950s: interpretive programs were not "fluff" or mere "icing on the cake," as was the view of many park superintendents at the time. Interpretation, Wirth believed, was at the very heart of the parks' preservation and protection mandate and was a vital part of the park service's congressionally sanctioned objective "to provide for the enjoyment" of parks and yet leave them "unimpaired" for the benefit of future generations. Tilden agreed; in later years he would write that "it has always been my philosophy to *protect first* and to *interpret second*," and if the goals of protection and interpretation could be mutually achieved, so much the better.

Convinced of the logic behind this underlying philosophy of interpretation, Wirth issued a directive to all the park service's field offices in April 1953 that gave interpretation a lasting mission: "protection through appreciation, appreciation through understanding, and understanding through interpretation." No longer was interpretation relegated to the back burner; henceforth, it was to be a vital part of the overall strategy of park management. But the director did not stop there. He put his philosophy in place organizationally in 1954 when he reshuffled his central Washington, D.C., headquarters to achieve this objective. As a consequence, a "Division of Interpretation" was created, not several echelons down on the Washington office's organizational chart but under the director's immediate supervision.

Tilden's observation that interpretation could use improvement meshed well with Wirth's grand plans for the MISSION 66 initiative. In October 1954 the NPS drew Paul Mellon's Old Dominion Foundation into the MISSION 66 project by requesting a $30,000 grant in "support of a research program designed to reappraise the basic principles underlying historical and natural history interpretation in the National Park Service." Assistant Director Ronald Lee, who oversaw the interpretation division, had an even more specific objective. He wanted the grant funds to be used "to get beneath the surface of method and procedure to the underlying principles—to the art and philosophy that should guide efforts to interpret the great scenic and historical heritage of America to her citizens." In reality, Mellon's grant was designed to support Freeman Tilden's special project—a multiyear venture to breathe new life into park interpretation. By February 1955 (the same month that MISSION 66 was formally inaugurated) the Old Dominion Foundation's board of trustees had approved the grant request, and shortly thereafter Tilden was off to the parks to begin in earnest his study of park interpretation.

WRITING *INTERPRETING OUR HERITAGE*

Though Tilden was no novice at interpretation, to fully grasp its underlying philosophy he visited scores of national park units, both natural and historical. He personally gave interpretive programs—what he termed "experiments"—at several parks, the most noteworthy being at the Castillo de San Marcos National Monument in Florida. He visited great natural areas, smaller historic areas, and state and privately owned heritage areas. At the Farmers Museum at Cooperstown, he observed craft "demonstrations." At Colonial Williamsburg and the Custis-Lee Mansion in Virginia, he experienced historic re-creations and reenactments—visitor experiences that he characterized as "animation," which is perhaps a more apt term than their modern-day designation as "living history." The generous funding provided by Mellon also allowed Tilden to attend numerous national and regional interpretive gatherings and conferences. Attendees recalled that at those meetings, Tilden, then seventy-two years old, actively engaged in the discussions, presenting what seemed to some to be rather original ideas about the interpreter's craft. He also advanced ideas for guiding principles that he was mulling in his mind, ideas that eventually would take shape as his famed six principles of interpretation.

The Old Dominion Foundation grant also enabled Tilden to spend time mastering the fine art of interpretive exhibit and wayside writing—what Tilden, in *Interpreting Our Heritage*, terms "inscription." This indeed was "interpretive" writing, a distinctive style of communication that demanded special attention to clarity, accuracy, and conciseness. As a result, Tilden helped produce a series of new interpretive markers that were placed at key locations within Acadia and Grand Teton National Parks.

In preparing his manuscript, Tilden sought to provide readers with the essential philosophy that underlies the art of interpretation. He did not specifically design the volume to serve as a textbook for college instruction for students of natural and cultural interpretation; rather, because it also contained guiding principles for the interpretive craft, he intended for it to be read and truly *used* by the field interpreter. What Tilden wrote is timeless; then as now, the book is best if read and reread every once in a while. The six major principles, straightforward and easily remembered, were designed by Tilden to become second nature to field interpreters. He hoped that these principles would become so ingrained in the interpretive thought process that when giving programs, interpreters would instinctively rely upon them.

Tilden submitted the draft of his manuscript to Ronald Lee, who was delighted by it. A few years later, after Tilden's *Interpreting Our Heritage* began to be considered the "Bible" of the interpretive profession, Lee wrote to Tilden, stating that while the book had not "superceded the *King James Version* yet," it was "more in the category of— what do the Seminarians call it—how to preach a good sermon."

But not everyone in the interpretive division shared Lee's enthusiasm. "I wonder if in belaboring the idea of a new concept we are not attempting to set ourselves up as high priests of a new cult," wrote one critical reviewer. Concerns were expressed over Tilden's use of the term "interpretation" rather than "education" or "indirect education." "Personally, I wish there were a better word than Interpretation," wrote another reviewer, though in the end even this individual was forced to conclude that there just "isn't any better word." Tilden, he wrote, deserves to take the credit for "taking the only word we have and attempting a new definition."

With the NPS review complete, the manuscript was sent to the University of North Carolina Press for publication. Once published, the NPS purchased 2,500 copies for distribution and internal use within the units of the National Park System. The final "thought-provoking report" was also forwarded to the trustees of the Old Dominion Foundation. Conrad Wirth, in his glowing foreword to the first edition, summed up the views of the NPS directorate: "We are delighted that so discerning an observer, and so able a writer, as Mr. Tilden has given us the full benefit of his observations and reflections. . . . This book is a splendid contribution toward providing the enjoyment that Congress had in mind when the system was created."

While the book received attention within NPS interpretive circles, it was not widely distributed. Fred M. Packard, executive secretary of the National Park Association (forerunner of the National Parks Conservation Association), considered *Interpreting Our Heritage* "a masterpiece of eloquent expression" and consequently published a rave review in *National Parks* magazine. In a letter to Ron Lee, Packard stated that it was a book that "every ranger-naturalist and historian should keep by his bed table." Furthermore, he stated, "copies should be made available to every interpreter," and "if its concepts are translated into positive action by all of them, the interpretive program will be dynamic and imaginative."

Fearing that the hardcover books would be relegated to park museums or library bookshelves, Packard then wrote to Director Wirth and suggested having "an inexpensive paper edition" published, "so that every naturalist on your staff, and the many other people who could make good use of it, could afford a copy for constant use." While hardback first edition copies of the book are now collector's items, for fifty years *Interpreting Our Heritage* also has continued to be available in paperback. Since Tilden first wrote it in 1957, it has gone through three subsequent editions and scores of reprintings. With the exception of the addition of the last chapter, "Vistas of Beauty," which first appeared in the second edition, there have been no substantive changes to the text. Tilden needs no revision; his writing remains as perceptive and inspiring as ever.

After completing *Interpreting Our Heritage*, Tilden turned his attention to the state parks. For two years, his travels took him to virtually every state in the Union. His *The State Parks: Their Meaning in American Life*, which was published in 1962, served to draw attention to the importance of state parks in the national psyche. Collectively, Tilden's writings on national and state parks advanced the modern notion that America needed to focus on creating not just a system of national parks but a great national "system of parks"—federal, state, and municipal.

In June 1960, while writing his state park book, Tilden decided "with great regret" to take leave from what had in essence been a full-time consultant position for the NPS. When he tendered his resignation, Tilden wrote that he considered his work for the National Park Service to be the "high spot in my professional writing life." For years afterward he continued as a "collaborator"—lecturing, teaching, and writing occasionally on parks, conservation, and interpretation. While Tilden did scale back his activities with the park service, he periodically contributed short articles on interpretation to internal NPS publications as well as *National Parks* magazine; several of these thoughtful pieces are reproduced in this volume.

In 1970 NPS director George Hartzog assigned Walt Dabney, a twenty-three-year-old student trainee who was posted at Yellowstone National Park, to accompany the aging Tilden (who was eighty-seven at the time) on what was to be his third and undoubtedly last extended trip around the country. The purpose of this trip was twofold: first, to assess how the NPS could best respond to the energy crisis; and second, to collect materials for future writings on the parks. The eleven-month odyssey took the two men through some fifty parks. They crisscrossed the country from east to west, from Florida to Canada, and back again. Every night, Dabney scribbled in his journal musings, reflections, and verbatim entries that remain an unpublished treasury of Tilden wit and wisdom.

The thoughts gathered by Tilden during that trip resulted in the publication of a succinct and eloquent statement describing what the national parks are. Through the encouragement of then director Hartzog, Tilden penned his last work for the NPS, *Who Am I: Re-*

flections on the Meaning of Parks on the Occasion of the Nation's Bicentennial, an extended essay that was subsequently published by the NPS in 1975 in pamphlet form. In its pages Tilden reflected on the way Americans use the parks, "not merely for recreation," he wrote, "but for the discovery of the delicate entity that makes You You and Me Me."

In the mid-1970s, Tilden found that although he was an old man, he shared much in common with the younger generation—including a real concern about the future of the global environment. After his last grand tour, in talks before communication classes at the NPS interpretive training center at Harpers Ferry, Tilden began openly advocating to interpreters that they needed to address the environmental crisis in their public programs. To this end, Tilden sought to make the young rangers "cognizant of the fact that, no matter how proficient an interpreter may be in other respects, he cannot reach the mind of a visitor unless he is keenly aware of the 'air of disturbance' in the mind of the visitor" brought about by insecurity from what he termed the "environmental morass in which our boasted Technology has mired us."

Certainly, Tilden was not alone in expressing these views; they were shared by other, often more vocal environmental activists of the 1970s, who were especially worried about the impacts of overexpanding population, depletion of raw materials, overcrowded cities, waste, and pollution of air and water. Shortly after listening to President Richard Nixon deliver one of his State of the Union addresses, Tilden wrote to Hartzog and offered suggestions on what role the National Park Service could and should play in the environmental crisis—or, as he characterized it, in this "web of crises." In an uncharacteristically long memorandum to the director, Tilden expressed support for formalized environmental education (especially in the primary school grades), but he argued that addressing the problem cannot wait another generation. "We must reach *adults*, by spoken and written word" he wrote, and to that end, he advanced a "program of understanding as we have never known. . . . It is in the field of morals."

Tilden did not envision environmental education as a sequential pedagogical enterprise targeted at students as was then being practiced in the NPS. For him, environmental education meant the communication of an ethic. And while the NPS should not "teach morals as such," he believed the bureau could use its "vast natural and historical resources to show what true morals are." By doing so, urged Tilden, "we do not tell people what they *must* do, but what they *can* do; not what they *must* be, but what they *can* be; and this by working with nature instead of against nature, and by following nature's order, with man instead of against man."

The idea that Tilden conceptualized was, as he told Hartzog, a "larger concept of Interpretation" than the one he had developed in *Interpreting Our Heritage*. In order to give the term interpretation "a fuller meaning and a greater depth," it must include the education of adults. Tilden concluded, "We have the exhibits, we have the beauties and the wonders, we have the skills that can be greatly expanded and developed. It is a matter of education of *adults*, not of a generation to come: now."

What Tilden advanced was a clarion call for environmental awareness and activism targeted at adult national park visitors and not just students. This was a new idea, at least for some park interpreters and environmental education specialists. Exactly how interpreters were to best deliver "the call to action" Tilden never detailed, though he strongly advised against "preaching": "Something in the mind of the interpreter . . . can be transmitted, perhaps not directly, not in the same sense of preaching. . . . Discretion is called for here because people do not like to be preached to." But he believed that "if you have a well-rounded knowledge of these conditions that we face, you cannot fail to transmit it in *some manner*, although not directly, to the perplexed people." Tilden's call for action (in part at least) was advanced and explained in an enlarged edition of his book *The National Parks*. In that book Tilden also introduced readers to a word that was not yet in common usage then: "ecology."

Despite Tilden's pleas and protestations, the National Park Service continued to craft its formal environmental education programs and interpretive efforts around children and students. Tilden's lectures to park service rangers and interpreters did, however, continue to serve as a catalyst for far more aggressive interpretation at the field level. As a result, some interpretive rangers indeed did begin to target strong environmental messages at adults.

Freeman Tilden died on May 13, 1980, in Nashua, New Hampshire.

Tilden frequently talked to young National Park Service interpreters at the Stephen T. Mather Training Center in Harpers Ferry, West Virginia. (Photo by Dan Riss)

When he passed on, he left behind not only hundreds of disciples who had come in personal contact with him, but also a body of writings that today still serves to guide and inspire interpreters as they strive to be true to Tilden's central charge: to remain "steadfast in our efforts to reveal the truths behind the appearances."

Ray Nelson, Tilden's close friend and confidant and the director of the Mather Training Center from 1967 to 1970, in his eulogy told mourners that Freeman often referred to Archimedes' bold statement: "Give me a fulcrum and I will move the world." Of his friend, Nelson said, "Freeman Tilden did move the world. His fulcrum was the pen and during his nearly ninety-seven years he moved the world to a much better place."

TILDEN'S MASTERPIECE:
INTERPRETING OUR HERITAGE

Undoubtedly, Tilden's most influential book for the National Park Service was *Interpreting Our Heritage*. It not only encapsulates the underlying philosophy of the interpretive art; it also gives substance to the craft.

By no means, though, was Freeman Tilden the "father" of professional interpretation. That distinction perhaps rests with John Muir, whose scribblings in his notebook in 1871 are considered the first known reference to nature interpretation. The designation also could go to Enos Mills, whose *Adventures of a Nature Guide* (1920) is considered a foundation book for modern-day interpretation. Tilden's contribution was not to define "interpretation" as much as it was to codify its operating principles. Through his travels, observations, and interpretive "experiments," he managed to capture in *Interpreting Our Heritage* a consolidation of his findings—the principles behind the "best practices," so to speak, of the professionals he had observed in the field. In the pages of his book, he presents those findings in a concise form that has served to inspire and challenge generations of interpreters.

While there are probably as many definitions of interpretation as there are interpreters—one of the most recent being by the National Association for Interpretation, which stated that "interpretation is a mission-based communication process that forges emotional and intellectual connections between the interests of the audience and the meanings inherent in the resource"—Tilden's definition still resonates in its simplicity of expression but complexity of meaning. Tilden recognized that interpretation implied the existence of an interpreter who was the central catalyst for the visitor experience. Recognizing that, he defined interpretation as "an educational activity which aims to reveal meanings and relationships through the use of original objects, by firsthand experience, or by illustrative media, rather than simply to communicate factual information."

But one cannot confine Tilden's definition of interpretation to this one sentence; certainly he didn't. Though he worked on the concepts of interpretation for twenty-five years, Tilden confessed to the young Walt Dabney that as late as the 1970s (years after he wrote *Interpreting Our Heritage*) he still didn't know exactly what interpretation was. He told Dabney that he had written a lot of definitions but was "never completely satisfied with them." Dabney then noted Tilden's insightful offhand remark: "It's something individual, something that comes from knowledge and doing, but you've got to feel it."

The limitations of a single definition in part are overcome when one considers the implications of Tilden's guiding six principles. In fact, as the essays reproduced in this volume illustrate, Tilden's notions about the meaning behind the word "interpretation" and its implications for the art and craft evolved over his lifetime. For example, when Tilden wrote *Interpreting Our Heritage*, the environmental crisis of the 1970s was still in the future. I am convinced that had Tilden been given the opportunity to update his book, he would have included a chapter specifically on the importance of environmental education. To that end, and as we see in "An Interpretive Ideal," the final essay in this updated edition, Tilden was passionate about the need to educate not just children and students but also adults about what he deeply believed was a looming environmental crisis. He wrote: "Our parks are the greatest natural classrooms available. We must use them to teach people the basics of ecology. We've been doing this for a long time, but we've got to do it better and on a bigger scale."

Even though Tilden's six principles have special relevance for personal services interpretation within a national park setting, in fact they are just as relevant to interpretation at a state or municipal park, battlefield, historic house museum, or other historic site as they are to national park units. His principles are universal. They speak to us today every bit as eloquently as they did in 1957.

These, then, are Tilden's six principles:

1. Any interpretation that does not somehow relate what is being displayed or described to something within the personality or experience of the visitor will be sterile.
2. Information, as such, is not interpretation. Interpretation is revelation based upon information. But they are entirely different things. However, all interpretation includes information.
3. Interpretation is an art, which combines many arts, whether the materials presented are scientific, historical, or architectural. Any art is in some degree teachable.
4. The chief aim of interpretation is not instruction but provocation.
5. Interpretation should aim to present a whole rather than a part and must address itself to the whole man rather than any phase.
6. Interpretation addressed to children (say, up to the age of twelve) should not be a dilution of the presentation to adults but should follow a fundamentally different approach. To be at its best it will require a separate program.

Even though these words were written fifty years ago, for the professional park, museum, or site interpreter none of these principles are outmoded or outdated. Upon first reading them and then comparing them to Tilden's definition of "interpretation," the discerning reader may be struck by the seeming contradiction that Tilden conceptualizes interpretation as an "educational activity," yet he states in principle number four (perhaps the most important of the six) that the chief aim of interpretation is not "instruction" per se but "provocation." Tilden apparently drew the notion of "provocation" from Ralph Waldo Emerson's 1838 Divinity School Address, in which Emerson, in discussing "intuition," said: "Truly speaking, it is not instruction but provocation, that I can receive from another soul." One cannot help but conclude that Tilden's wide, varied, and learned readings gave him a broad, unobstructed view of the nature of instruction, communication, education, conservation, nature education, and environmental education.

TILDEN'S OTHER INTERPRETIVE WRITINGS: SOME ADDITIONAL PRINCIPLES?

Tilden was not wedded to only six principles; nor should we be. Years later, when asked by an inquisitive interpreter about how he had originally conceptualized his principles, Tilden answered that "there was nothing sacred about the number of principles being six." He thought "there may be twelve," or "perhaps, they could all be telescoped into one—love; love in a general sense, love for your own existence . . . love for people not persons . . . love of nature . . . [and] the love to communicate." To Tilden, the number simply was "not important."

Tilden's statement of principles has inspired scores of others to expound on his fundamental concepts, his words, his thoughts, and his philosophy. As an instructor at the Mather Training Center in Harpers Ferry, I well remember the discussions and at times heated arguments we had in class when course participants speculated on what should be Tilden's "seventh" principle.

Part III of this expanded commemorative edition of Freeman Tilden's interpretive writings contains five essays that have been drawn from the writer's collected works. Most were written after the publication of *Interpreting Our Heritage*. Though Tilden wrote on other aspects of the national and state park experience, only occasionally did he venture to once again put ink to paper and reflect on the philosophy and techniques of interpretation.

The essays in part III have come from a variety of sources. As stated previously, one was originally a chapter in a book by Tilden on the national parks. Two essays originally were contributions to *National Parks* magazine and targeted at a lay but knowledgeable audience; another is reproduced from the now-defunct NPS interpretive bulletin *Trends*. And one—the last essay (chapter 20)—was discovered in a dusty file folder in the NPS collections on deposit at the U.S. National Archives. When found, it was merely described as "Draft of Freeman Tilden's mss. for brochure on interpretation." I opted to give it the descriptive title "An Interpretive Ideal" because it set forth Tilden's views on what a natural or cultural park area's "comprehensive" interpretive experience should be like for visitors.

Readers will find these later essays lively and thought provoking. Several are written in a similar voice and tone, as is "Vistas of Beauty," the final chapter that Tilden added to the second edition of *Interpreting Our Heritage*. A few of the essays are stylistic gems. They reflect Tilden's love of parks, of nature, and of the interpreter's art. In several of them Tilden advances ideas sure to make contemporary interpreters think. For example, in "An Interpretive Ideal," Tilden suggests that national park visitors should be able to experience a traditional "campfire program"—not a syrupy or maudlin re-creation of the legendary and historically unfounded campfire discussion that supposedly gave birth to the national park "idea," or a tired slide presentation or time-filling educational video, but a program that provides a thoughtful, entertaining, and educational experience for visitors—one that is fundamentally drawn from the mind, experience, and wit of the interpreter. "This is the time," Tilden writes, "in such a gathering, that the interpreter can truly project the meaning of the natural world; the community of living things—bird, animal, insect, flower, and tree—and their part in our own human existence." Tilden then declares: "Every visitor should be provided, some way, with this classic campfire experience. It is a precious link with nature and the American story." Such programs, Tilden concludes, can and should serve "as the centerpiece" of an evening program at natural areas.

Each of the later essays, in addition to advancing some provocative ideas, may contain the seeds of yet another set of interpretive "principles." These, then, are some generalized principles that could be drawn from each essay (and readers may find still others):

1. From "Mindsight": beauty and revelation are not always obvious or even seen. What lies behind what the eye sees is far greater than that which is visible.
2. From "That Elderly Schoolma'am": interpretation addressed to special populations at times means that special sensory-based interpretive techniques or programs become necessary in order to help visitors connect with the resource.
3. From "The Constructive Aspect of Inaction": beauty perceived

by the organs of sense often needs no interpretation; nature's handiwork readily interprets itself.

4. From "Two Concord Men in a Boat": interpretation is a means, in Thoreau's words, "to wake my neighbors up" and move them to action.

5. From "An Interpretive Ideal": a primary end goal of interpretation is to help the visitor understand his or her personal obligation to heritage protection and preservation.

Whether these principles drawn from Tilden's later interpretive writings are on target or misguided, or possibly just plain wrong, I leave to the discerning reader.

One final note: in editing Tilden's essays, I have used a light editorial hand. Tilden was a fine writer—you can hear his voice in his words. Nevertheless, as readers of *Interpreting Our Heritage* have commented, his style was, as I characterize it, "generationally determined," and as such he tended to refer to interpreters and others in the masculine. Every effort has been made to preserve and not unnecessarily intrude on the integrity of his thought and style. Typos were corrected and slight copyediting changes were made, but only to incorporate modern usage and bring stylistic consistency to the various editorial formats used by the original publishers.

R. BRUCE CRAIG
Prince Edward Island, Canada
Easter Sunday 2007

Part I

I have been careful to retain as much idiom as I could,

often at the peril of being called ordinary and vulgar.

Nations in a state of decay lose their idiom, which loss is

always precursory to that of freedom. . . . Every good writer

has much idiom; it is the life and spirit of language: and none

such ever entertained a fear or apprehension that strength

and sublimity were to be lowered and weakened by it. . . .

Speaking to the people, I use the people's phraseology.

— Demosthenes to Eubulides,

  in Imaginary Conversations, *by Walter Savage Landor*

CHAPTER 1

🖋 Principles of Interpretation

The word "interpretation" as used in this book refers to a public service that has so recently come into our cultural world that a resort to the dictionary for a competent definition is fruitless. Besides a few obsolete meanings, the word has several special implications still in common use: the translation from one language into another by a qualified linguist; the construction placed upon a legal document; even the mystical explanation of dreams and omens.

Yet every year millions of Americans visit the national parks and monuments, the state and municipal parks, battlefield areas, historic houses publicly or privately owned, museums great and small—the components of a vast preservation of shrines and treasures in which may be seen and enjoyed the story of our natural and man-made heritage.

In most of such places the visitor is exposed, if he chooses, to a kind of elective education that is superior in some respects to that of the classroom, for here he meets the Thing Itself—whether it be a wonder of nature's work, or the act or work of man. "To pay a personal visit to a historic shrine is to receive a concept such as no book can supply," someone has said; and surely to stand at the rim of the Grand Canyon of the Colorado is to experience a spiritual elevation that could come from no human description of the colossal chasm.

Thousands of naturalists, historians, archaeologists, and other specialists are engaged in the work of revealing, to such visitors as desire the service, something of the beauty and wonder, the inspiration and spiritual meaning that lie behind what the visitor can with his senses perceive. This function of the custodians of our treasures is called interpretation.

Because of the fear of misconception arising from conflicting definitions of the word, and also because some have thought it a pretentious way of describing what they believe to be a simple activity, there has been objection to the use of the word "interpretation" even among those engaged in this newer device of education. For myself I merely say that I do not share this objection. I have never been able to find a word more aptly descriptive of what we middlemen, either in the National Park Service or in any institution employing the means, are attempting to do.

But all during the practice of this educational activity, whether science or art or something of both, there has existed a strange situation. Interpretation has been performed—excellent, good, fair, and unsatisfactory—with only a vague reference to any philosophy upon which interpretation could be based.

I have heard some superb interpretations not only in the National Park Service areas, but in far lesser places, and have found by interrogation that the interpreter was aware of no principles, but was merely following his inspiration. I actually believe that if there were enough pure inspiration in the world to go around, this might be the best way to perform the service. But we are not so cluttered with genius as all that. You have only to attend some of the worse performances in interpretation to wish heartily that there were some teachable principles, and perhaps some schools for interpreters.

This book results from a study of interpretation as practiced in the many and diverse cultural preserves I have mentioned and from an inquiry as to whether there is such a philosophy, whether there are such basic principles, upon which the interpreter may proceed with an assurance that, though he may not be inspired, he will do an adequate job.

Since the earliest cultural activities of man there have been interpreters. Every great teacher has been an interpreter. The point is that he has seldom recognized himself specifically as such, and his interpretation has been personal and implicit as a part of his instruction. In a sermon called "A Christmas Message," Harry Emerson Fosdick showed what seems to me a profound knowledge of the highest meaning of this word, in speaking of Jesus. He said: "There are two kinds of greatness. One lies in the genius of the gigantic individual who . . . shapes the course of history. The other has its basis in the genius of the *revealer*—the man or woman who uncovers something universal in the world that has always been here and that men have not known. This person's greatness is not so much in himself as in what he unveils. . . . [T]o reveal the universal is the highest kind of greatness in any realm."

The reason why our college graduates, in past decades, have spoken with such reverence and affection of certain of their teachers—

such men as Copeland and Charles Eliot Norton of Harvard and Bumpus of Brown, to name just three among many—was because such men by universality of mind instinctively went behind the body of information to project the soul of things. One of his pupils said of Dr. Bumpus: "He thoroughly enjoyed his stay upon this planet, which he found so full of a number of things . . . and he enjoyed pointing out these things in a new light. . . . He never forgot that the *feeling* of an exhibit and the need for it to tell a story were quite as important as its factual truthfulness."

To take a slice of a tree like the giant sequoia, and to associate its growth rings with a time chart of our human history, was an idea that occurred to some master interpreter.

Since interpretation is a growth whose effectiveness depends upon a regular nourishment by well-directed and discriminating research, this introductory chapter seems as good a place as any to stress the importance of that resource. In an article printed in the magazine *Antiques*, Edward P. Alexander of Colonial Williamsburg, speaking of historic preserves, wrote: "Research is a continuing need and the life blood of good preservations. Both historical authenticity and proper interpretation demand facts. Research is the way to obtain these facts. There is no substitute for it, and no historic preservation should be attempted without research."

Colonial Williamsburg itself offers an ideal example of this truth. Here it is possible, through the generosity of Mr. Rockefeller, to employ the skill and taste of the most competent researchers in many fields to the end of bringing to life accurately and beautifully a segment of our early American history.

In the National Park Service is found an abundance of proof of the statement, and not merely in the department of history. Research is responsible for the satisfactory and stimulating experience of the visitor to Crater Lake, where the interpretation takes the visitor beyond the point of his aesthetic joy toward a realization of the natural forces that have joined to produce the beauty around him. This experience is made possible through continuing research here, because the explanation first accepted of the origin of the mighty caldera was not that which is now generally held. Nor was the research at Crater Lake alone that of the geologist. Many other specialists, including the archaeologist, had their part in revealing the facts.

Visiting a historic shrine is a unique, sometimes life-changing experience.
(Courtesy of National Park Service)

To stand at the rim of the Grand Canyon is to experience a spiritual elevation
that could come from no human description of that colossal chasm.
(Courtesy of National Park Service)

The vivifying programs at the Custis-Lee Mansion in Arlington, Virginia, emerge from the painstaking efforts of the historian who was not content with large generalizations but sought in the records of the two families a multitude of homely details that bring the Custises and Lees into touch with our own daily experience.

At Fort Necessity, associated with the young George Washington, "something was wrong with the picture," as we say, yet cursory observation and guess had failed to arrive at the facts. Indeed a palisade reconstruction had been based upon false premises. A park service archaeologist who refused to give up, even though many times baffled, was finally able to depict this tiny frontier post as it really was.

It had been commonly said for many years that the Nelson bighorn sheep had entirely disappeared from the confines of Death Valley National Monument. Indeed, so it was believed by practically all except the sheep themselves, whose rather important numbers now are made a matter of fact through the efforts of a naturalist, Ralph Wells, who has "lived" with flocks of the animals in the furnace-hot summer of the valley.

Dinosaur National Monument comes to mind readily in this regard; so, naturally, does Jamestown, where digging in preparation for the Exposition of 1957 made it finally possible to people that little first settlement of the English-speaking colonists and gave the ancient inhabitants flesh on their bones and blood in their veins.

When I consider what competent research can do in a yawning void, my mind goes to Fort Frederica, in Georgia, for it is natural for us to draw upon impressions that are gained at first hand. Previous to the work of the archaeologist, teamed with the historian, at Oglethorpe's colony on the sea-island near Brunswick, I attempted some volunteer interpretation there at a time when there was not sufficient personnel present to aid the visitors. Charming as was that ancient ruin, with its live oaks and soothing estuary frontage, I found it almost impossible to make it real. I knew the historical background well enough, but the eyes of the visitors constantly wandered from me. I knew what they were thinking: "What was it like?" The structural relics were not imposing. The mounds might be those of earthwalls, but they did not register.

Well, I went to Frederica again, after the diggers had uncovered the site of the Hawkins-Davison houses, and again I had the pleasure

Careful research is the foundation of the interpreter's art.
(Photo by Dan Riss)

Ruins like these at Chaco Culture National Historic Park often serve as the catalyst for visitors to glimpse the past. Here, as in every interpretive activity, the chief aim of interpretation is not instruction but provocation. (Courtesy of National Park Service)

of telling the story of Frederica to certain groups. What a difference those bricks and those exposed walls made! Somebody had lived here; this was part of a town, it now had a being.

Some years ago, in scrambling up a steep hillside of the Jemez Mountains of New Mexico, I found the ground well strewn with petrified marine shells of several species. I was at an elevation of not less than 7,000 feet. The discovery did not surprise me in the least; but it did make me wonder what the prehistoric Americans who must have seen such shells had thought about them. I knew that I was standing somewhere near the shoreline of a shallow sea that occupied this spot at a time before the land had been slowly upraised. How did I know this? The story had been interpreted for me; seemingly unrelated facts had been reasoned into a whole picture that solved all difficulties.

❧ For dictionary purposes, to fill a hiatus that urgently needs to be remedied, I am prepared to define the function called interpretation by the National Park Service, by state and municipal parks, by museums and similar cultural institutions as follows:

An educational activity which aims to reveal meanings and relationships through the use of original objects, by firsthand experience, and by illustrative media, rather than simply to communicate factual information.

This, let me emphasize, is for the dictionary, which logically attempts only an objective definition of words as they are, or have been, commonly accepted. The true interpreter will not rest at any dictionary definition. Besides being ready in his information and studious in his use of research, he goes beyond the apparent to the real, beyond a part to a whole, beyond a truth to a more important truth.

So, for the consideration of the interpreter, I offer two brief concepts of interpretation, one for his private contemplation, and the other for his contact with the public. First, for himself: interpretation is the revelation of a larger truth that lies behind any statement of fact.

The other is more correctly described as an admonition, perhaps: interpretation should capitalize mere curiosity for the enrichment of the human mind and spirit.

In the matter of definition, I have tried to arrive at something upon which we can fairly well agree. We are seldom entirely happy with the utmost pains of the lexicographer: we find words given as synonymous that we do not so consider; a definition is too inclusive, or it fails to emphasize that which we believe is vital. As to the concepts given above, I should hope that the interpreter will have others of his own, doubtless just as valid and just as stimulating. If we can agree upon principles, the stress and shading of the individual will be no impairment but a reflection of his true appreciation of those principles.

Now, what are these principles? I find six bases that seem enough to support our structure. There is no magic in the number six. It may be that my reader will point out that some of these principles inter-finger. It may be that he will feel that, after all, there is but one, and all the others are corollary. On the other hand, since I am plough-ing a virgin field so far as a published philosophy of the subject is concerned, some of my readers may be provoked into adding further furrows. Very well. This book pretends to no finality, no limitation. We are clearly engaged in a new kind of group education based upon a systematic kind of preservation and use of national cultural re-sources. The scope of this activity has no counterpart in older nations or other times.

I believe that interpretive effort, whether written or oral or pro-jected by means of mechanical devices, if based upon these six prin-ciples, will be correctly directed. There will inevitably be differences in excellence arising from varied techniques and from the person-ality of the interpreter. Obviously I cannot be concerned with those factors in such a book as this. The National Park Service has an exten-sive manual and a number of admirable booklets for the governance of the spot-conduct of both the interpreter and his interpretation.

Here, then, are the six principles:

1. Any interpretation that does not somehow relate what is being displayed or described to something within the personality or experience of the visitor will be sterile.
2. Information, as such, is not interpretation. Interpretation is revelation based upon information. But they are entirely different things. However, all interpretation includes information.

3. Interpretation is an art, which combines many arts, whether the materials presented are scientific, historical, or architectural. Any art is in some degree teachable.
4. The chief aim of interpretation is not instruction, but provocation.
5. Interpretation should aim to present a whole rather than a part and must address itself to the whole man rather than any phase.
6. Interpretation addressed to children (say, up to the age of twelve) should not be a dilution of the presentations to adults but should follow a fundamentally different approach. To be at its best it will require a separate program.

I plan to make no generalizations in this book without the support of one or more illustrations or examples. My aim is clarity and succinctness, rather than style, even though I recommend that the interpreter never forget that "style" is a priceless ingredient of interpretations. "What is style?" somebody asked of a French writer. "Le style, c'est l'homme," was the reply. (Style is just the man himself.) So style is just the interpreter himself. How does he give it forth? It emerges from love. We shall later have a little chapter upon love. I do not name it here as a principle. It is, indeed, not a principle but a passion.

CHAPTER 2 🪶 **The Visitor's First Interest**

As we read, we must become Greeks, Romans, Turks, priest, king, martyr and executioner; must fasten these images to some reality in our secret experiences. —Ralph Waldo Emerson

---

Any interpretation that does not somehow relate what is being displayed or described to something within the personality or experience of the visitor will be sterile.

A roster of the reasons why people visit parks, museums, historic houses, and similar preserves, though a fascinating excursion into human psychology, need not detain us here. All interpreters know from their experiences that the reasons are so many and diverse that merely to name them all would take pages of this book.

I go upon the assumption that whatever their reasons for coming, the visitors are there. What we should determine, then, if we aim at establishing our first principle of interpretation is: now that the visitor is here, in what will be his chief interest, and inevitably his chief interest, while he is with us?

The answer is: the visitor's chief interest is in whatever touches his personality, his experiences, and his ideals.

The adult visitor who happens to be the auditor or reader of interpretation has no general awe of the interpreter. He takes it for granted that the latter possesses special knowledge that he himself lacks, and he respects both that knowledge and the possessor of it (especially if he is in uniform) to exactly that extent. But he is not without his pride, or vanity if you wish, and he probably considers himself just as good an "all-around man" as his interlocutor. He does not so much wish to be talked *at* as to be talked *with*. He knows, and the interpreter knows, that this is not directly possible. It cannot be a round-table conversation. Hence we have to try to achieve something of this purpose in some oblique way. In a moment we shall see that there is definitely such an indirect means.

But first, as to the intimation that the visitor's chief interest is in something that concerns himself. This attitude of the adult is not to be confused with what we commonly know as selfishness. It not only is not the same thing—it need not even have much in common with it.

Professor C. E. Merriam in his book *The Making of Citizens* has indicated the strength of the urge of men to associate themselves with the historic past:

> The underlying design is of course to set up a group of the living, the dead, and those who are yet unborn, a group of which the individual finds himself a part and of which he is in fact glad to count himself a member, and by virtue of that fact an individual of no mean importance in the world. All the great group victories he shares in; all the great men are his companions in the bonds of the group; all its sorrows are by construction his; all its hopes and dreams, realized and thwarted alike, are his. And thus he becomes although of humble status a great man, a member of a greater group; and his humble life is thus tinged with a glory it might not otherwise ever hope to achieve. He is lifted beyond and above himself into higher worlds where he walks with all his great ancestors, one of an illustrious group whose blood is in his veins and whose domain and reputation he proudly bears.

I once referred to interpreters, speaking of those in the National Park Service, as "middlemen of happiness." Of course, it is impossible for anyone to make someone else happy. "Le bonheur n'est pas une chose aisée," said Nicholas Chamfort. "Il est très difficile de le trouver dans nous, et impossible de la trouver ailleurs." (Happiness is not easy to come by. It is hard to find it within ourselves, and impossible to find it anywhere else.) Neither the sublime qualities of the primitive national parks, nor anything the interpreter can say about them, can make anyone happy; but the one and the other, happily teamed, can offer those elements by which people can bring to life their hidden capacities for happiness.

Generally speaking, certainties contribute toward human happiness; uncertainties are a source of spiritual loneliness and disquietude. Whether or not he is conscious of it, man seeks to find his place in nature and among men—not excluding remote men. Primitive parks, the unspoiled seashore, archaeological ruins, battlefields, zoological and botanical gardens, historic sites—all happen to be exactly those places where this ambition is most likely to be satisfied. So, even though your visitor may not himself know just what immediate impulse brought him to any one of these places, he is for this ultimate reason in a receptive mood. To capitalize this mood, even if it arises from mere curiosity or whim, is a challenge to the interpreter.

The visitor is unlikely to respond unless what you have to tell, or to show, touches his personal experience, thoughts, hopes, way of life, social position, or whatever else. If you cannot connect his ego (I use the word in an inoffensive sense) with the chain of your revelation, he may not quit you physically, but you have lost his interest. Dr. John Merriam spoke of "that touch of presentation . . . which relates it to personal interest." When a person reads a novel or sees a play, he instinctively measures the fictional behavior against what he imagines his own character and conduct, under such circumstances, would be.

In the museum, the interpreter can seldom come into contact with his visitor. In lieu of that, he must leave a message for him. Usually this will take the form of a label. Most interpreters have heard the statement of Dr. Brown Goode that "a museum is a well-arranged collection of labels, illustrated by specimens." I assume this to be a deliberate exaggeration to emphasize a truth. But the label certainly can be galvanic, or it can be inert. The label can project itself directly into the personality of the visitor to the exhibit, and make him feel a direct connection with what he sees. Two good examples of this I found in the Witte Museum in San Antonio, Texas. One label was on a large case that contained the skeleton of a mammoth: "Prehistoric mammoths were here in Texas just a few thousand years ago. They roamed the plains in great herds. . . . The chances are that they browsed right where you are standing now."

Where *you* are standing *now*. With that statement the mammoths are not far away creatures of time or space but right under your feet. Another gem from the same museum—this time on a case showing West Texas plants that were used by aboriginal Indians. "Do you need a water bucket? a pair of shoes? a blanket, floor mat or rope? If so, the materials in this case [sotol, lechuguilla, bear-grass, devil's shoestring, etc.] will serve your purpose."

As he reads this label, and views these plants, the visitor is no longer wholly a foreigner to the prehistoric man. *He* would have

Sometimes the underground world can seem alien to visitors. At Carlsbad Caverns interpreters accept the challenge of helping visitors relate to what for many is an unfamiliar part of nature. (Courtesy of National Park Service)

The ancestors of millions of visitors fought in the Civil War. To tread on the same ground where their forefathers fought connects visitors with their pasts. (Photo by R. Bruce Craig)

had these needs. He would have supplied these needs with exactly these materials. He and they are brothers-under-the-skin. Certainly it would not be well to overwork this word "you." It would become offensive. There are plenty of ways to effect the same end. If labels can merge a plant exhibit with the personality of the visitor, surely the interpreter can do far more to that end when he has the privilege of direct contact.

A felicitous example of the knack of associating the object with some homely but keen sense of drama that lies within the visitor's personal range is to be found at the Franklin Delano Roosevelt home-site in Hyde Park, New York. It is in the room where the President was born. You could put up a label and say, "President Roosevelt was born in this room." That is accurate information. Or in personal contact with his group the interpreter would be at liberty to state the fact in any elaborated way he might please. But someone had an inspiration here. What you see is a reproduction of the telegram sent by the happy father, James Roosevelt, to a friend announcing the arrival in Hyde Park "of a bouncing boy, weight 9½ pounds, this morning." It is just what you or I would have done, and you instantly feel kinship not merely with the Roosevelts, but with the whole mansion and area.

For remember, the visitor ultimately is seeing things through his own eyes, not those of the interpreter, and he is forever and finally translating your words *as best he can* into whatever he can refer to his own intimate knowledge and experience. I put the words *as best he can* in italics, because thus it will emphasize the importance of making this translation as easy as possible. Words like dendrochronology and photosynthesis and biota, and excursions into Latin taxonomy, not merely do not aid him, they throttle him. If, indeed, there were time to reveal the picture-quality of some of these apt technical words, they might appeal to the few, but I fear that the interpreter faces enough difficulties without further adding to them.

In most of what the interpreter may tell a visitor of prehistoric or modern man's activities, at peace or at war, the opportunity always arises to provoke in the mind of the hearer the questions, "What would *I* have done under similar circumstances? What would have been *my* fate?" Is the visitor at Lee Mansion, across the Potomac from Washington? Robert E. Lee never occupied this house for long. But in it was the scene of the great tragic moment when a man who loved the Union, and the United States army he had served, had to make a decision. Virginia was his mother. What should he do? What, given all the circumstances, would the visitor have done?

It may not be too much to say that most history may be interpreted effectively (but of course not exclusively) by provoking the thought, "Under like conditions what would *you* have done?"

Perhaps the visitor is being told of the atlatl, the throwing stick of the Southwest prehistoric Indian. Would the visitor have found out and applied a principle of physics that enabled him to "lengthen his arm," so to speak? Well, many of those visitors as children sharpened the end of a stick, thrust it into a green apple, and then hurled the apple much farther than they could have thrown it with the unaided arm and hand. That was a throwing stick, was it not?

Dr. Clark Wissler once said, "As a rule the visitor entering Mesa Verde the first time has no conception of prehistoric life in the Southwest. Everything looks strange and unexpected." Now, imagine the visitor to have come to a prehistoric Indian ruin on Thanksgiving Day, after a typical modern dinner. He would probably have been eating turkey, squash or pumpkin pie, and possibly corn bread or corn in some other form. At least sixteen articles of food in our present-day menu have come down to us from these aboriginal peoples, according to Dr. John Corbett. Here, for the visitor, is at once offered a vivid link with the past. Skillful interpretation goes on from there into homely parallels with our own day-to-day existence. These people of other centuries played, loved, quarreled, worshipped, knew beauty— all the essentials were about the same. The strangeness and unexpectedness mentioned by Dr. Wissler disappears. The visitor says, "These folks were not so different, after all."

Finally, so far as this chapter is concerned, I hope to clinch the nail with what I regard as a triumph of interpretation by Thomas Henry Huxley, one of the greatest of biologists.

Huxley engaged to deliver a series of lectures to Workingmen's Institutes in certain English cities. One of these talks was delivered in Norwich. Huxley called it "On a Piece of Chalk." It was such a superb bit of composition that it became a classic of English style and appears in many anthologies. We are now not concerned with the style, but only with its superiority as interpretation. Here are Huxley's opening words: "If a well were sunk at our feet in the midst of the city of Norwich, the diggers would very soon find themselves at work in that white substance almost too soft to be called rock, with which we are all familiar as 'chalk.'"

Consider this beginning—very free and easy, conversational, without a single suggestion that the speaker is one of the world's great men of science. The audience is immediately made a part of everything that is to follow. The well may be sunk right under where they are sitting. It will be *their* well, not a well in East Prussia. It is therefore *their* chalk. Only later will they learn that this bed of chalk extends 3,000 miles to central Asia.

"A great chapter of the history of the world is written in the chalk." A little tug on the imagination, but not too much. Huxley brings it back home again: "Every Norwich carpenter carries a bit of this chalk in his pocket."

"The language of the chalk is not hard to understand. Not nearly as hard as Latin, if you only want to get at the broad features it has to tell." Notice that phrase "it has to tell." Not "I want to tell you something you ought to know," but "the chalk will tell you something."

Now comes the masterpiece: "I propose that we now set to work to spell that story out together." From that moment, everything Huxley is going to tell his audience (and most of it was entirely novel to them) is going to be like a discovery they are about to make, with Huxley going along as a sort of companion.

〰 "The world exists," said Emerson, "for the education of each man. There is no age, or state of society, or mode of action in history, to which there is not something corresponding in his own life."

CHAPTER 3 🌿 Raw Material and Its Product

The simple fact that a great battle was won or lost makes little impression on our mind . . . while our imagination and attention are alike excited by the detailed description of a much more trifling event. . . . This must ever be the case while we prefer a knowledge of mankind to a mere acquaintance with their actions.
—Sir Walter Scott, in introduction to Froissart

Information, as such, is not interpretation. Interpretation is revelation based upon information. But they are entirely different things. However, all interpretation includes information.

The National Park Service has, for the guidance of its personnel, an exhaustive administrative manual. A section of this manual deals with "Information and Interpretation in the Field." Speaking of "Newspaper Publicity" at the area level, one of the injunctions to the employee is as follows: "Do not editorialize in a news story. Stick to statements of fact, which can include the fact that somebody, identified in the story, expressed an opinion which is germane to the story."

Of course this would be accepted by anyone as prudent advice. It means, in effect, do not try to interpret: merely inform.

Let me try to give an illustration of how this policy works out in the case of the newspaper itself. When Adolph Ochs was the owner and manager of the *New York Times*, he took what may be termed a purist attitude as to the place of information and interpretation in his newspaper. To him, it was not proper that his reporters should go beyond writing the facts, so far as it is humanly possible to ascertain the facts. Interpretation of the news belonged to the editorial page. It is inescapable that a reporter, who after all is a human being, could not altogether avoid imprinting his personality upon even a cold recital. But this was the ideal of the *Times* under Ochs.

Exactly the opposite view, in the newspaper world, was that of Dana and Laffan of the *New York Sun*. The reporter was not merely given leave, he was encouraged, in the interest of readability, to "make a good story" of an event. As a result the *Sun*, which was often called a newspaperman's newspaper, always sparkled, while the writing fraternity, even though they respected the Ochs ideal, called the *Times* colorless.

The San Francisco earthquake of 1906 supplied a fine test of the two journalistic points of view. For many hours the stricken city was cut off from the world. In such a case, dependence is always upon rumor, opinion, and stray leakage of "facts" (usually not facts at all). The *Times* strove diligently in its news columns to maintain its ideal. But the *Sun* had on its staff a brilliant newspaperman named Will Irwin, who was a San Franciscan. The "news" story written by Irwin will always be a classic of journalism. The earthquake facts did not bother Will. All he knew was that his beloved city at the Golden Gate was broken and burning. He and his brother Wallace (also a writer) had been happy there in the fleecy fog that rolled in, of afternoons, down to Van Ness Avenue; they had feasted joyously at the Poodle Dog in its palmy days; they had jinked with the Bohemians. Will poured out his heart in a "story" that interpreted the very essence of his city. People that had never been there felt that they, too, had leaned against a lamppost on Market Street, and had idled in the picturesque Chinese quarter around Grant Avenue. They saw, felt, and heard—and lamented the loss of something that had instantly become theirs. This was interpretation: the revelation of the soul of a city. It was based upon fact, but they were not the facts of the earthquake destruction. I imagine Mr. Ochs of the *Times* enjoyed this Irwin tour de force as much as anyone, but he might not have printed it. He believed that information was one thing and interpretation was another, and seldom the twain should meet.

It is an idle quibble to point out that the interpreter may, and indeed in most cases must, dispense pure information; or that, conversely, the man who gives information may indulge in words that are actually interpretive. The same dual role can exist in the roadside sign or the label and normally should be present in printed matter. It is only necessary to keep in mind that they are dual roles; that information and interpretation are essentially two different things.

When Charles Darwin was a young man, he made a voyage of nearly five years in a British warship. The account of that circumnavigation of the globe was published under the title of *The Cruise of the*

Beagle and has become so much a classic for the lay reader that it is included in Everyman's Library. Many a person who has never gone through *The Origin of the Species* or the *Earthworm* has taken delight in the *Beagle*.

In this book, Darwin shows that the man of science can be also a great interpreter, with a subtle sense of what is needed to make scientific discovery and research come alive to the average man. His picture of the degraded natives of Tierra del Fuego has almost fictional allure.

In South America Darwin was at one time in the Uspallata Range of the Cordilleras. He described the topography and the geology of this area—straight information. "It consists," he wrote, "of various kinds of submarine lava, alternating with volcanic sandstones and other sedimentary deposits . . . from this resemblance to the tertiary beds on the shores of the Pacific I expected to find silicified wood." He did find such wood; they were firs, of the Araucarian family, with some affinity to the yew.

Thus far, this was information, and specialized. You could not expect the layman to become very enthusiastic about the statement. But Darwin proceeds.

It required very little geological practice to interpret the marvellous story which this scene at once unfolded. . . . I saw the spot where a cluster of fine trees once waved their branches on the shores of the Atlantic, when that ocean came to the foot of the Andes.

I saw that they had sprung from the volcanic soil which had been raised from the level of the sea, and that subsequently this dry land, with its upright trees, had been let down into the depths of the ocean. In these depths the formerly dry land was covered by sedimentary beds and these again by enormous streams of submarine lava. . . .

But again the subterranean forces exerted themselves, and I now beheld the bed of that ocean forming a chain of mountains more than 7,000 feet in height . . . nor had the antagonist forces been dormant, which are always at work wearing down the surface of the land: the great piles of strata had been intersected by many wide valleys, and the trees, now changed into silex, were exposed projecting from the volcanic soil, now changed into rock, whence formerly, in green and budding state, they had raised their lofty heads. Now, all is utterly irreclaimable and desert; even the lichen cannot adhere to the stony casts of former trees.

If anyone points out that in this graphic interpretation of the facts Darwin was still employing certain words that would be unfamiliar to many readers, that is true. But it must be remembered that the words were meant to be read, not spoken, and book reading implies the opportunity to look up words in the dictionary, when the interest is excited. At any rate, it seems to me a grand example of interpretation, manifesting the differences between what is informative and what is interpretive. When Darwin used the word "interpret," he showed plainly that he, at least, never confused the two things.

Robert F. Griggs of Ohio State University, the leader of the Mount Katmai expeditions of 1915 and 1916, gave in his fascinating article written for the *National Geographic Magazine* a perfect example of that felicitous touch of interpretation that relates the unfamiliar to the familiar in the mind of reader or auditor.

Katmai had erupted in June 1912. It was one of the most tremendous volcanic explosions of all time, as may be judged by the estimated five cubic miles of ash and pumice belched into the air. But Katmai was far away, even the name being unfamiliar to most people. To say what the effect of this eruption was upon the country around it would be likewise speaking of a vague territory sparsely inhabited. But Griggs found a way to make it real.

Imagine, advised the writer, a "similar outburst" centered in New York City. "In such a catastrophe all of Greater New York would be buried under ten to fifteen feet of ash and subjected to the unknown horrors from hot gases. The column of steam would be plainly visible beyond Albany. . . . Philadelphia would be covered by a foot of gray ash and would grope in total darkness for sixty hours. Washington and Baltimore would receive a quarter of an inch. . . . The sounds of the explosion would be heard as far as Atlanta and St. Louis. The fumes would be noticed as far as Denver, San Antonio and Jamaica."

This device of interpretation, brought home, could be used in giving an adequate notion of the magnitude of our great Columbia Basin lava flow. Pick up that lava, so to speak, and lay it down east of the Mississippi, where the concentration of population and development is greatest. "Here is what, if it happened now, it would bury and destroy . . ."

In his book called *Life on the Mississippi*, Mark Twain, in the very first chapter, showed that he knew what interpretation is. After stating that De Soto saw the river in the year 1542, Twain wrote:

> To say that De Soto saw it in 1542 is a remark which states a fact without interpreting it: it is something like giving the dimensions of a sunset by astronomical measurements and cataloguing the colors by their scientific names—as a result you get the bald fact of the sunset, but you don't see the sunset.
>
> The date standing by itself means little or nothing to us; but when one groups a few neighboring historical dates and facts around it, he adds perspective and color. . . . For instance, when the Mississippi was first seen by a white man, less than a quarter of a century had elapsed since Francis I's defeat at Pavia; the death of Raphael, the death of Bayard . . . Catherine de Medici was a child; Elizabeth of England was not yet in her teens . . . Shakespeare was not yet born.

There is not room here to reproduce the whole long paragraph. It is enough to say that (as was Twain's intent) after you read the list of associated events, you have perspective: the year 1542 has ceased to be merely a calendar entry.

Certainly the raw material of interpretation is information. My quotations from Huxley, Twain, and Griggs have shown that the researcher himself may be a fine interpreter. But this is only to say that some men can play dual roles superbly. It is not a just expectation of the scientific worker that he should be expert in both the science and the art. The interpreter begins where the decision has finally been made: "This is what we think proper to call the facts."

There are cases where, after long study, the specialists are not agreed as to what are the facts. "What," asked Dr. Schroeder of me one day, "are you going to do, as to your public interpretation, where two competent archaeologists draw opposite conclusions from a body of evidence?" My answer is that the person engaged in interpretation (the kind with which this book deals) must wait for authoritative decision from some source. Sometimes, where good authorities differ, he may well present both sides. When the matter is of such tremendous import that he must tell a story about it, as in the case of the Pleistocene glaciation, he may frankly say that nobody knows the precise answer; such an occasional statement sometimes produces a feeling of added confidence in the hearer.

In Acadia National Park, aside from the scenic land-and-sea beauty, the visitor is primarily interested in the many physical evidences that the land was once deeply covered by a slowly moving sheet of ice. There are many hypotheses as to what caused this glaciation in North America and Europe; none is, of itself alone, satisfactory. In such a case, true interpretation need not be hampered. Indeed, the visitor, after being frankly informed that nobody knows the ultimate cause, may be induced (we are all challenged by puzzles) to do some thinking about it himself; even if his thinking is unscientific, his horizon cannot fail to be widened. In a region of the blind a one-eyed man may become king.

The work of the specialist, the historian, the naturalist, the archaeologist, is fundamental, then. Without their research the interpreter cannot start. But you sometimes note an impatience on the part of a specialist that the public does not show sufficient interest in his assemblage of information as such. He is likely to conclude that the average person is somewhat stupid. The opposite is true. It is a sign of native intelligence on the part of any person not to clutter his mind with indigestibles. "We find it to be a law," said James Garth Wilkinson, a great English surgeon, "when a branch of knowledge has been cultivated for ages and still remains inaccessible to the world at large, that its principles are not high or broad enough, and that something radically deeper is demanded. If it does not interest universal man, that is sufficient to prove the point."

The "something radically deeper" is an art form—an analogy, a parable, a picture, a metaphor—something that "brings things down and incarnates them," as Wilkinson said. This art form, for our purpose, takes the shape of interpretation.

Comprised within the National Park System, as well as within state and other historic sites, are many places that must carry to the visitor some broad impression of the toil, the sacrifice, the intelligence, and the conflict that is part of our national history. Let us take, for example, the cluster of Civil War battlefields and related areas. In the fifty years following the end of that fratricidal war, there was much emphasis, when the veterans and their children were visiting the scenes of each bloody combat, upon information. It was then a thrill to know, to recall, just where papa's regiment had stood, by what road an advance or retreat was made. It is true, of course, that under the circumstances then existing, the mere recital of information could have been in some degree an interpretation.

Now that we approach the centenary of the outbreak of the war, it becomes increasingly clear that the visitor's interest is not so much in the military details, but in the great human story: "Why did men act as they did? How would I act under such circumstances? What does it all mean to me?"

It is true that there are exceptions to this general statement. The historian in one of these areas must be prepared to deal with the informative as well as the interpretive. A group of Civil War Round Table enthusiasts will be interested in specific details of a battle; so will students preparing a paper; so may younger school groups where the visit is intended to reveal, perhaps, the part played by the troops of a state or locality. But these are the exceptions, and insofar as they are, they are not interpretation. Jacques Barzun, the historian, has stated the case boldly and well:

> However stupid or uneducated, the most indifferent citizen will remember and respond to certain ideas connected with his country's past. Lincoln's log cabin may suggest the heroism of western pioneers or it may mean that humble birth is no bar to high office. . . . To a Frenchman you need not explain Joan of Arc. The intricate details of her career, trial, and death, are as nothing compared with the image that spells patriotism, kingship and sainthood.

"The historian," continues Barzun, "who forgets his duty is the one who attempts the treatment of an actual historical question and thinks he has achieved it when he has only rummaged into the past and exhibited his finds. . . . The use of History is not external but internal. Not what you can do with history, but what history does to you, is its use."

Finally, I wish to quote something from B. H. Liddell Hart, in a preface to his book on General William Tecumseh Sherman:

In places such as Valley Forge National Military Park,
history may be interpreted effectively by provoking the thought,
"Under like conditions what would I have done?"
(Courtesy of National Park Service)

Those accustomed to the conventional history and biography may complain that the account of battles is uncomfortably bare and scantily furnished with details. . . .

To place the position and trace the action of battalions and batteries is only of value to the collector of antiques, and still more to the dealer in faked antiques. . . . This book is a study of life, not of still life. An exercise in human psychology, not in upholstery.

I do not subscribe to the tone of asperity employed; but I think the comment not only has merit but sharply points out that true interpretation deals not with parts, but with a historical—and I would say spiritual—whole.

The professor threw himself down upon the sofa and moaned: "I am a
hopeless failure as a teacher."
"This is just the dejection of a moment, my dearest," said his wife,
gently. "Why should you think yourself a failure?"
"It is not momentary. I have seen it for some time. For months my pupils
have shown an interest in everything I tell them."
A great joy shone in the woman's eyes. "I have known it always," she
cried. "You are a poet! I am so happy you have found it out at last.
We shall now starve happily together."
—Pedro Sarráchaca, El Pedagogo Vascongado

Interpretation is an art that combines many arts, whether the
materials presented are scientific, historical, or architectural.
Any art is in some degree teachable.

Sooner or later the interpreter must face the question of whether
he is dealing with a science or an art. Interpretation is one or the
other; it cannot be both. If it is an art, it can draw upon all science.
But if it is a science, it can have no patience with "the sweet insou-
ciance of lettered ease." Dr. John Merriam remarked of Albert Michelson, the physicist, that "it was his lot to be a scientist, otherwise he
would have been a great artist." The very fact that Michelson chose to
be the one rather than the other is sufficient to indicate that in practice they are not compatible.

Someone—perhaps Whitehead—referred to education as "knowledge treated imaginatively." Science cannot afford to treat knowledge
imaginatively in the sense that the artist can, though great scientists
are men of high imagination. So, if you regard education as a science,
the only way the educator can achieve such an end is to turn to art.
The teacher of arithmetic must insist that two and two make four.
H. G. Wells proposed that there is actually no such thing in life as
"two." Therefore, he said, the truth is that "a little more or less than
two plus a little more or less than two, equals a little more or less

than four." Wells was speaking as an artist. He was treating knowledge imaginatively. The public accountant will go right on insisting that bookkeepers had better avoid art, except as an avocation.

"Use materials as the basis for education," said Merriam, "but treat them imaginatively." You cannot treat the materials imaginatively without giving them form. This is what Heinrich Heine had in mind when he lamented, concerning his fellow Germans: "Thanks to the conscientious exactitude with which we are bent, we compilers never think about the form that will best represent any particular fact."

Merriam implied, when he used the word "education," a much higher service than the teaching of facts. He yearned, in our national parks, for an appeal to the emotions, to the hunger for deeper understanding, to the religious spirit of the individual, no less than to the love of beautiful and wonderful objects, or the restoration of physical well being.

> I can't attempt to tell you what I think about Nature. Probably your reactions are like mine. But the point is . . . that the contribution of science gives a vision of the continuity of law which looks like a purpose in Nature, that makes our relation to Nature—all the way from contact with the clod to the tree or to the mountain—in one sense that of companionship. I am inclined to think that the poets have come closer to the appreciation of what this means than any other group of people.

It will be obvious at this point where we are driving. We have already given up the notion that interpretation, in the sense we are employing the word, is direct education. Now, then, we may as well plump it right out. The interpreter must use art, and at best he will be somewhat of a poet. This sounds frightening, I allow. I can see some of my readers shuddering at the thought and wondering where it leaves them. "But I never wrote a line of poetry in my life. You cannot expect me to be an artist."

I reply: you do not know yourself. You have been so frustrated by the curatorship of unimportant details that you have forgotten your inborn talent. We are all, in some degree, poets and artists. If you mean you are not capable of the exquisite flights of a John Keats or the rumbling organ tones of a Thomas Hardy, very well. None of us are. But we can have something of the perception of a poet without having the graphic skill. We can have a sense of joy at sounding a lovely chord, without being a virtuoso.

I once made a long automobile trip with a businessman. We had been on the road only a few hours when I came to the sour conclusion that the adventure was a mistake for both of us. Either he was prosaically dull or I was intellectually a bore, or both. I could elicit nothing but sodden commonplaces from him. It was developing into a mobile nightmare. But we finally came to western New England—the Berkshire Hills—and it was springtime. My companion had never been that far east before. He suddenly stopped the car on a hillside and sat for a moment looking at the white birches, with greening leaves. Then he said, "Look! Those trees seem to be all racing down the hill to wash their feet in the creek." And, reacting to his poetic impression, I began to see exactly what he saw. Out of this humdrum John had popped something as lovely as an old Greek myth.

If a nymph had appeared it would not have surprised me.

You just never can tell how much artistic perception people may have in their depths. The interpreter who uses art, creating a "story" out of his materials, will find himself in the presence of people who have the artistic appreciation to understand him.

I am sure that what I am saying will not be misconstrued to mean that the interpreter should be any sort of practicing artist—that he should read poems, give a dramatic performance, deliver an oration, become a tragic or comic thespian, or anything as horribly out of place as these. Nothing could be worse, except perhaps to indulge in an evangelical homily. I am merely suggesting that he dip into his own artistic appreciation, give form and life to his material, and tell a story rather than recite an inventory. The whole history of entertainment reminds us that a dull performance has a dull audience; and while we must be chary of that word "entertainment," and be sure we restrict ours to the very highest kind, we cannot forget that people are with us mainly seeking enjoyment, not instruction.

The makers of the ancient myths, as G. K. Chesterton reminds us, cultivated the "images that were adventures of the imagination," and "they best understood that the soul of a landscape is a story, and the soul of a story is a personality."

What makes me sure that I am right about this is the fact, so well known to me, that there are many interpreters in the National Park Service who have come to such a conclusion, perhaps before I myself did. Harry C. Parker wrote me some years ago (in guarded terms, fearing I might misunderstand him), "I sometimes believe that interpretation . . . is more of an art than a science." Merrill Mattes ventures a modest belief that "to do a really good job, a writer must have an instinct for compression of words found mainly among poets and advertising men." The "instinct for compression" is, after all, just another way of describing form. The artist ruthlessly cuts away all the material that is not vital to his story.

I have heard so many wise statements concerning the necessity for "telling a story" from interpreters now within the National Park Service that for a long time I have wondered why they did not put their own convictions into their practice. I can only suppose that they have been reluctant to be thought innovators. But if, indeed, they have not been quite convinced that they were right, I hope that my affirmation will give them as much courage as theirs has given me.

It is probably true that the professional writer will always be able to score more hits in the production of interpretive literature, of markers and labels, than the nonprofessional. At the same time the professional can sometimes be so hypnotized by his own skill and by his affection for phrasing that he touches only the brain and does not reach the heart. For that reason, I wholly agree with James W. Holland when he says that excellent texts might sometimes be written by "a superintendent or a clerk, an engineer or a ranger, or even a member of the maintenance force." Therefore, I likewise partly agree with J. C. Harrington that "many now in the Service could do an adequate job—if they could and would take the time." I regard interpretation as a teachable art; therefore I do not think it is at all a matter of "taking time." All the time in the world is insufficient unless the principles are understood. All the good intentions are unavailing unless the interpreter understands that form is the essence, and that pedagogical miscellany is a bore to the man on holiday.

To the specialist, the use of metaphor is calamitous, and simile is almost an obscenity. Analogy may be employed, but only for the purpose of further perplexing a student. I am not saying that, within his limited educational orbit, the specialist is not right about this. I rather assume he is. But he must realize that this abhorrence of artistic form is exactly why, in speaking to a lay audience, he can empty a room more quickly than a cry of "Fire!"

The lifeblood of satisfying interpretation flows from the proper and ingenious use of exactly those devices of language that take the hearer or reader beyond the observed fact to, or at least toward, a certification of spirit. "I disbelieve," said Garth Wilkinson, in ringing tones that are fit to be engraved on the memory of every interpreter, "in what is called the severity, strictness, and dryness of science . . . we have found practically that metaphor is a sword of the spirit, and whenever a great truth is fixed, it is by some happy metaphor that it is willing to inhabit for a time: and again, that is whenever a long controversy is ended, it is by one of the parties getting hand on a metaphor whose blade burns with the runes of Truth."

The King James version of the Bible, which has been the model of many a master of simple and effective composition, is a storehouse of these "burning blades." Abraham Lincoln's Gettysburg Address flows straight from his youthful devotion to this marvel of English style. Suppose Mr. Lincoln had devoted an hour at Gettysburg to a closely reasoned and brilliant analysis of the relative strategy of Meade and Lee. Do you think his talk would now have been graven on bronze?

You may have had the experience of going out for an evening and having your host, or perhaps your hostess, begin to regale the party with "a story you will be interested in." Something that really happened to us last August—or was it September? We were on our way to—where was it, Emily? No it couldn't have been that place; that was another time. The story drags along, with interruptions caused by recalling this queer thing about Uncle Henry, and that perfectly gorgeous view from a mountaintop in where-was-it—no, that was the year before. The narrative begins to bog down in a welter of details that couldn't possibly be associated with any story that had any point or ending. Finally the narrator himself bogs down and flounders hopelessly: "Now, where was I?" You no longer care where he was; you only care about where you would like to be—home. He has used a mountain of material to slay one mouse that might have really been a story.

But listen to a skilled raconteur. He knows exactly where he is going when he starts. If he brings in what appears to be divergence, you quickly discover that it is important to the matter. He excludes every word and phrase that does not lead directly to his ending. And mark this: he does not necessarily mind if you perceive the inevitable conclusion before he gets there. The most successful stage plays may not be those that keep the audience in the dark till the final curtain. On the contrary, if the audience begins to guess correctly the outcome, from that point they may be doubly gratified: they now have the pleasure of being clever enough to share in the art of working it out.

The interpreter who creates a whole, pares away all the obfuscating minor detail and drives straight toward the perfection of his story will find that his hearers are walking along with him—are companions on the march. At some certain point, it becomes their story as much as his.

It should be clear, from the foregoing, that while the interpreter is called upon to employ a combination of the arts, his main reliance will be upon a proficiency in what we call rhetoric; that is, the art of writing or speaking. Especially, it implies skill in the presentation of ideas, adapted to whatever situation is at hand.

CHAPTER 5

🕊 Not Instruction but Provocation

The arts of education that will summon the people to learn are . . .
different from and greater than those which have been sufficient for
the schools. . . . It is in fact powers of attraction in knowledge that
are demanded for the new education. In the first place, attractive
knowledge gains the learner and keeps him. In the second place it
enlarges his genius, and out of that, his memory, whereas dry knowledge
cultivates his memory at the expense of his mind. In the third place
such knowledge is coherent with itself . . . giving the learner a constant
sensation that he is developing it for himself, which lets him into the
legitimate delight of mental power. —James John Garth Wilkinson

---

The chief aim of interpretation is not instruction but provocation.

Instruction takes place where the primary purpose of the meeting between teacher and pupil is education. The classroom is the outstanding example of this, but it can apply to field and factory work as well. When, as early as 1899, college professors were beginning to take their students into areas that afterward became national parks, their purpose was instruction. The students were not there primarily to look at scenery, to relax, or to contemplate.

In the field of interpretation, whether of the National Park System or other institutions, the activity is not instruction so much as what we may call provocation. It is true that the visitors to these preserves frequently desire straight information, which may be called instruction, and a good interpreter will always be able to teach when called upon. But the purpose of interpretation is to stimulate the reader or hearer toward a desire to widen his horizon of interests and knowledge, and to gain an understanding of the greater truths that lie behind any statements of fact.

The national park or monument, the preserved battlefield, the historic restoration, and the nature center in a public recreation spot are exactly those places where interpretation finds its ideal opportunity, for these are the places where firsthand experience with the objects of nature's and man's handiwork can be had.

Ansel F. Hall, then chief naturalist of the National Park Service, delivered a message "to all park educational officers" in 1928, and I quote it here because it early made clear something that was afterward misunderstood by many interpreters—that neither the function nor the aim of our interpretation is instruction:

In most Park educational activities it is best to give the visitor a broad, general idea of the Park in which he finds himself, allowing him to supplement the general but inclusive story with details according to his personal impressions of the facts which he himself gathers out-of-doors. He may gather these perhaps with your assistance, but he must be stimulated first to *want* to discover things for himself, and second, to *see and understand* the things at which he looks. . . . Remember always that visitors come to see the Park itself and its superb natural phenomena, and that the museum, lectures, and guided trips afield are but means of helping the visitor to understand and enjoy these phenomena more thoroughly. . . . A few believe it is our duty to tell as many facts as possible, and therefore take pains to identify almost every tree, flower and bird encountered. Others have taken as their motto "to be nature minded is more important than to be nature wise," and feel that it is more important that the visitor carry away with him an intense enjoyment of what he has seen, even though he has not accumulated many facts.

As Ralph Waldo Emerson had written many years before, "Truly speaking, it is not instruction but provocation that I can receive from another soul."

In a book upon the principles of interpretation it would be not only ungenerous, but actually a deficiency, to fail to consider the brilliant and unselfish efforts of the group of men that launched the educational program that, to a considerable degree, still remains the essence of National Park Service interpretation. Far from being an afterthought, the National Park Service was born with this ideal of employing the beauty and wonder of the parks, and the leisure that permitted visitation, as a sylvan path toward reverence and understanding.

It seems to have been a clear policy in the mind of Stephen T. Mather when he became the first director. As one of his earliest steps

Beauty of and for itself needs no interpretation. Later, questions will come. "What great natural forces lie behind all this?" Then the interpreter's moment has arrived. (Courtesy of National Park Service)

in implementing this policy, he persuaded Mr. and Mrs. Charles M. Goethe, of Sacramento, to transfer to Yosemite National Park the venture in nature guidance that they had helped initiate earlier at Lake Tahoe. Their interest in such activity had been aroused after observing similar activities in their travels abroad. Mr. Mather gave warm encouragement also to Jesse L. Nusbaum's early interpretive activities at Mesa Verde National Park.

Unfortunately there is not room here to recount all the fine spadework done in interpretation between 1916 and 1928. Following these early activities, the secretary of the interior appointed a committee to make a thorough study of educational possibilities in the national parks, the expenses of the survey to be met by a donation from the Laura Spelman Rockefeller Memorial Fund. This group, consisting of John C. Merriam, Hermon C. Bumpus, Harold C. Bryant, Vernon Kellogg, and Frank R. Oastler, went into the field and produced a preliminary report full of practical suggestions for "promoting the educational and inspirational aspects of the Parks."

During the following year three others, Clark Wissler, Wallace W. Atwood, and Isaiah Bowman, were added to the first group, constituting an Educational Advisory Board to the National Park Service; and in ensuing years more field investigations were conducted in the parks and monuments. The final report pointed out "responsibilities and opportunities for education and research in the fields of history, earth sciences and life sciences," and laid down a program.

The early part of the background of interpretation in the National Park System has been summarized in a booklet, *Research and Education in the National Parks*, by Dr. Harold C. Bryant and Dr. Wallace W. Atwood Jr. (1932), and in *The History and Status of Interpretive Work in National Parks*, by Dr. Carl P. Russell (1939). I wish that these papers might be available to interpreters generally, because they do so much more than the mere narration of the early work in this field. Personally I agree with the suggestion in the park service administrative manual that "Research and Interpretation" would best express the aim.

Finally, in 1953, as part of a reorganization plan for the National Park Service, with a view to strengthening the work of interpretation in the field, a new division was created in the Washington office, with a chief of interpretation directing and coordinating the work of the branches of History, Natural History, Information, and Museums. In addition, each of the five regional offices has its interpretation chief with a staff including a naturalist, a historian, a biologist, and an archaeologist.

With the giving of this brief background of the constant movement toward a more coherent and understanding program for interpretation in the National Park System, I shall now look back a little upon the thoughts and feelings of the early workers in the field. Naturally these educators were concerned primarily with the educational possibilities in the scenic and scientific parks and monuments; in later years the system was to be augmented by the addition of a great number of historic and prehistoric monuments, variously designated, but all presenting chapters in the American Story. However, if I am correct in assuming that there is a philosophy of interpretation, and basic principles upon which adequate interpretation can be built, the nature of what is being shown and illumined makes no difference. Interpretation is interpretation anywhere, anytime.

The title of the booklet that emerged from the labors of the early educators, *Research and Education*, was, strangely enough, misleading. Neither research nor instruction is of itself interpretation. Yet each of the men involved in the survey was perfectly conscious that the desirable end was what we are now calling interpretation. Again and again in their individual reports they expressed thoughts that clearly showed that they had a keen sense of an underlying philosophy. I have no question that Merriam or Bumpus, for instance, if they had chosen, could have stated the principles of interpretation with clarity.

The explanation is this: the members of the committee were bent upon formulating a plan for educational endeavor in the parks that could be put into some sort of practice at the earliest possible moment. They were aiming to fill what they considered, and Stephen Mather considered, a lamentable void. They pointed at that which could be readily understood in the field by field men. The enunciation of a body of basic principles could wait.

The plan was sound and admirable. It was comprehended, in its import, by many in the field. But others were unduly impressed by the word "education." The word, coming from well-known educators, suggested direct and detailed instruction. Thus, in so many cases that we have observed, the provocation to the visitor to search out meanings for himself, and join in the expedition like a fellow discoverer, was sometimes submerged in a high tide of facts, perfectly accurate, perfectly ineffectual.

My experience is that the groups of people who seek out interpretation in the areas of the National Park System are wonderfully well mannered and pathetically eager for guidance toward the larger aspects of things that lead toward wisdom and toward the consolations that come from a sense of living in a natural world and a historic continuity that "make sense." And as a participant in such groups I have so many times had my enthusiasm wilted by an interlocutor who mistook information for interpretation—who became a poor instructor when he could have been an inspiring guide.

But mark how Dr. Merriam understood it. Consider these paragraphs from him:

> The wider the range of observation and of thought on the part of the visitor, the greater the opportunity for what Henry Van Dyke described as "being lifted up through wonder into joy."

> The mind of the adult requires more certain foundations in reality; it demands a clear exposition of relationships and definitions of perspective.

> There is danger that we study only the stones, that were left from parts of the buildings of the Maya, forgetting that they represent a people still living in the region.

> There comes to me the story recently told by a friend who went out into one of those most remote corners of the Navajo Reservation to a place that some of you have seen in the Canyon de Chelly; that is, the White House. He was not able to go up this magnificent canyon because the sand was too deep. So they rode on horses along the edge of that magnificent cliff, with its roseate rocks that reflect the light of the sun in a most extraordinary way, and finally they came out on a high point. There they looked across the sandy wash to the eight-hundred-foot cliff on the other side, in the bottom of which in those great recesses were these magnificent buildings of ancient times known as the White House. And they stood there

for a long time looking at this perfectly magnificent work, with the background of nature behind it. And then a Navajo came out from a little side canyon and stood on a rock in front of the White House and sang a song; and my friend said: "From the whole of my experience in that long trip this was the most magnificent thing—the story of man, with the great background of geology behind it, and then the expression of a living being illustrating the thought and the life of the people." And I said, "Why was that so wonderful to you?" And he thought a while and said, "I do not know."

Well, let us see if we can give the answer. Was it not, very simply, that the act of the Indian gave life to a picture that was otherwise beautiful but inert because it was unrelated to anything within the experience of the beholder? Was this not a fine instance of accidental interpretation?

Not the least of the fruits of adequate interpretation is the certainty that it leads directly toward the very preservation of the treasure itself, whether it be a national park, a prehistoric ruin, a historic battlefield, or a precious monument of our wise and heroic ancestors. Indeed, such a result may be the most important end of our interpretation, for what we cannot protect we are destined to lose. I find in the park service administrative manual a concise and profound statement, and my heartiest thanks go to whoever it was that phrased it: "Through interpretation, understanding; through understanding, appreciation; through appreciation, protection."

I would have every interpreter, everywhere, recite this to himself frequently almost like a canticle of praise to the Great Giver of all we have, for in the realest sense it is a suggestion of the religious spirit, the spiritual urge, the satisfaction of which must always be the finest end product of our preserved natural and man-made treasures.

He that understands will not willfully deface, for when he truly understands, he knows that it is in some degree a part of himself. "I do not wish to fling stones at my beautiful mother [nature]," said Emerson, "nor soil my gentle nest. I only wish to indicate the true position of Nature in regard to man, wherein to establish Man, all right education tends." It must be a bold person who would dare to amend our greatest American philosopher and interpreter, but I must dare it just this once. It is clear that Emerson was so intent upon the

The Liberty Bell has special meaning for all. Interpreting it can reveal deeper truths—what Tilden characterizes as "the soul of things." (Photo by R. Bruce Craig)

perfection of man that (for the moment) he failed to realize that nature and man are inseparable companions. They are one. If you vandalize a beautiful thing, you vandalize yourself. And this is what true interpretation can inject into the consciousness.

But not with the mere recitation of facts. Not with the names of things, but by exposing the soul of things—those truths that lie behind what you are showing your visitor. Nor yet by sermonizing; nor yet by lecturing; not by instruction but by provocation.

Not long ago I was one of a caravan that made a trip through one of the national parks. The leader, the interpreter, was a seasonal ranger, a college professor from another part of the country who had been returning to this park for several years because he loved it. In the course of three and one-half hours (too long) this ranger took his group from one place to another. It was a hot day, and I was by turns amused and chagrined by his method—if it was a method. He violated almost every accepted rule of technique in dealing with his group. He horrified me by dealing largely in Latin taxonomy. Yet in the course of that hot and dusty trip the tired feet of the visitors stayed with him, and I began to see why it was. It was love. This seasonal man loved passionately every manifestation he was showing and describing; he transmitted that love and translated it to understanding.

Finally, standing upon the top of a bald mountain, this man gave me the last surprise. As fresh as though we had just started our tour, he told a thrilling story of the way the rock under our feet was attacked by the physical and organic forces; how vegetation begins; the creation of little harboring places in the rocks; the coming of grasses, of shrubs, finally of trees. Our grasses, our forests. The tired crowd followed with rapt attention. Then suddenly, after pointing out the centuries upon centuries that it takes to create such verdure and such beauty, he concluded abruptly, with a gesture and snap of the fingers: "And with a lighted cigarette *you* can destroy it all—LIKE THAT!"

Dramatized? Yes. Overdramatized? No. It was perfect. Not all the warning signs about fires ever put on the roadsides, not all the statistics ever published, not all the logic ever spoken, could have had the effect that this ranger secured upon his group. I say his group, because admittedly the occasion, in conservation, was special. We do not often have that chance.

But the point remains. It was not instruction. It was provocation.

CHAPTER 6

🪶 Toward a Perfect Whole

Interpretation should aim to present a whole rather than a part and must address itself to the whole man rather than any phase.

Of all the words in our English language, none is more beautiful and significant than the word "whole." In the beginning it meant "healthy." I believe the thought it expressed was that no human being could be healthy who was well only in certain parts of his physical and moral self. "They that be whole need not a physician" (Matt. 9:12.) I believe there is not one of us who, looking back upon the errors of his own life, can escape the conviction that most of these were caused by mistaking a part for a whole. It is easy to do, for the contemplation of a part supplies an enjoyment of the understanding, while the search for the whole is hard work. "I see it all," we are inclined to say, when the fact is that we have not perceived the truth at all.

A cardinal purpose of interpretation, it seems to me, is to present a whole rather than a part, no matter how interesting the specific part may be. It will be observed that I say "a" whole, not "the" whole. "The" whole soars into infinity, and the time we can spend with our listener or reader is all too brief. A friend of mine said to me, "The tourist has three limitations—of time, of absorptive capacity, and of money." Truly: so it becomes the more important to make of his contact an appreciation of a whole rather than of any part.

Imagine yourself in the presence of a visitor from some other planet. He has heard of a bird, but he has never seen one. You know a great deal about birds. You will perhaps want to tell him that the wing of a bird, in anatomy, is very much like the arm of a man, or the front leg of a horse, or that it even has its counterpart in a fish. Then the bird, as insect eater, is a friend of the farmer; and as food some of the birds are much sought by hunters. You could tell him a hundred interesting facts about birds, ending with that lovely artistic concept of John Rushkin, that "the bird is little more than a drift of air brought into form by plumes." Your visitor would be left wondering what a bird was like. A bird is a small whole, not an assembly of parts and attributes. If you don't think this is true, I beg you to take your parts and attributes and make me a bird.

At first glance, when I speak of a perfect whole, it may seem that I am indulging in a counsel of perfection—something extremely difficult for the interpreter to achieve. I believe the contrary to be true. It is exactly when, in an address to a group, the repeated interpretation tends to deal with a collection of discrete facts that both the audience and the interpreter himself become bored and listless. We all view with horror the possibility of what we call a stereotyped performance. Such a cliché is almost impossible when the interpreter has, either by intuition or by plan, managed to convey a dramatic whole.

Since intuition cannot be generally trusted, it follows that the interpreter must proceed from a principle, and the principle is this: it is far better that the visitor to a preserved area, natural, historic, or prehistoric, should leave with one or more whole pictures in his mind than with a mélange of information that leaves him in doubt as to the essence of the place, and even in doubt as to why the area has been preserved at all. To illustrate what I mean, I shall give an example derived from each type of preserved area mentioned.

First, from a primitive region, whether set aside for its beauty or its scientific qualities, or for both: Big Bend National Park. This is a desert-mountain-river wilderness, redeemed from a certain amount of former commercial use, and intended, so far as visitor access and accommodation may permit, to revert to its natural condition. Here a great dissected mountain mass of igneous rocks rises out of a plain that slopes toward the Rio Grande. Seen from the viewpoint of naturalist, historian, and archaeologist, there are thousands of interesting facts that can be told about what has happened here.

One of the stories here is the desert story. The spacing of the creosote and cactus growth in the lower lands is noticeable. The giant daggers are unique and impressive. The lovely agaves march up the sides of the Chisos Basin and burst into their swan song of flower at the age when they will sacrifice themselves for their species. There is a weeping juniper in the mountains that exists only in this Texas region, so far as North America is concerned. The highest peaks are forested with trees that you would expect to find much farther north in latitude.

What, then, among so many features that cannot possibly be absorbed in a tourist visit, may be a *whole* that would stir the imagination, leave an indelible impression, and lead the visitor to wish to know more about the subtle adaptations of organic life? What you see here is a story of diminishing rainfall, or rather, of precipitation. There has been a "flight" from increasing aridity over the many centuries. If you, the visitor, have come here from a region that receives forty inches of rain and snow a year, this is what, in general aspects, your land would look like, and the way the organic life would be forced to behave, if the rain clouds became reluctant. I do not promote this particular whole. The spot interpreter can judge better than I can. I merely say it is a whole.

Let us go to Vicksburg National Military Park. This Civil War shrine has great natural beauty, since it rests upon the deep fertile loess of the Mississippi bank. But presumably the visitor is here because of the dramatic long siege that resulted in the surrender of the city to Ulysses S. Grant on Independence Day in 1863. This was one of the most involved operations of the war. If the interpreter were to have hours with his hearers, instead of minutes, he could not possibly exhaust the details of the manifold and fruitless attempts that were made to capture the stronghold from the river side. Grant's finally successful investment from the land side covers an almost equally involved series of military successes for the Union.

Here, again, there are wholes of far more meaning to the present-day visitor than the military strategy and tactics. A whole is found in the story of Missouri, as revealed in this siege and capture. The 11th Missouri Regiment, USA, was on one side of the fighting; the 3rd Missouri, CSA, was on the other. From that fact is illumined the human tragedy that was the war itself: fratricide. It reveals the story of a divided border state, with an animosity almost exceeding that of Deep South and North. What difference does it make now, except to the researcher, who commanded these regiments? Or whether they were stationed on the left or right? Some of these Missouri boys, now striving to kill each other, were once fed gingerbread and doughnuts from the same Aunt Nellie's jar. That is a whole. Likewise the stark tragedy of Lieutenant General John C. Pemberton—the apostate

Participation is a valuable ingredient of interpretation.
By providing opportunities for personal interaction with the resources,
the interpreter encourages visitors to interpret for themselves.
(Courtesy of National Park Service)

northern man who threw in his fortunes with the southern cause, and became the very general who was forced to surrender the bastion—is a whole.

I happened to be at one of the smaller southwestern national monuments, Tonto, not far from the Roosevelt Dam in Arizona. While I was talking with the ranger-naturalist there he said to me, apropos of nothing in particular, "You know, Mr. Tilden, most of the people who come here look at that steep hillside up which the Indians climbed when they came back from their fields, and think life must have been a great hardship for those people. But I think they lived the life of Riley!"

I replied, "That seems to me a whole. I hope you'll weave that into a picture for the visitor who doesn't care whether the pottery was white on black or black on white, or who is not greatly exercised as to whether the migration into America came across the Bering Strait or by rafts to South America."

Of course, these prehistoric folks at Tonto had their ill moments, like people anywhere else. But at best it must have been a habitation of great pleasure, with few wants, the bright Arizona sky over them, and no hurry. The visitor himself, similarly placed and conditioned, would have done exactly everything these people did, perforce in almost the identical way, and he would have loved it, and thought his home the center of the earth, his children the best children, his gods the best gods. This is a whole, and though we owe such a debt of gratitude to the patient study of the archaeologist, he must always remember that his tools are not the public's tools, nor his scholarly thoughts their thoughts. Hear what our Concord sage said of this:

> All inquiry into antiquity is the desire to do away with this wild, savage and preposterous There and Then, and introduce in its place the Here and Now. Belzoni digs and measures in the mummy-pits and pyramids of Thebes, until he can see the end of the difference between the monstrous work and himself. When he has satisfied himself . . . that it was made by such a person as he, and to the ends to which he himself should also have worked, the problem is solved.

Samuel Whittemore Boggs, the geographer, once spoke of "the wholesomeness of wholeness." When I first considered the statement, I was inclined to think the phrasing a bit overstrained. I now understand that Boggs was profoundly accurate. The wisest man is insufficiently conscious of the remedial quality of mere presence in the wilderness when he first comes from the marketplace of nerve-wracking half-truths and no-truths into a genial haven of a whole. Then as the jaded and shredded man senses the unmarred fabric of life all around him, he begins to feel himself becoming whole again. This is a phase of that "wholesomeness."

It is the same if he visits the scene of Washington's birthplace on Pope's Creek in Tidewater Virginia. The house he enters is not the house where George Washington was born, but the spirit of our great whole man is there; and in these lovely and provoking surroundings, the staunch character of our hero comes to the imagination. Out of related and even unimportant facts emerges, at the instance of true interpretation, that greater truth, that all-important image—the character of the undaunted leader of the Revolution. The visitor takes hold upon himself. What Washington was in great, I can at least be in my little. These were the virtues of a whole man. I can safely aspire to be a whole man, too, though I am no Washington. It was this that Boggs called wholesomeness and wholeness.

For this and similar reasons the interpreter, whether in wilderness places or in historic houses or in the museum, must always make his appeal to the whole man that the visitor represents. This may seem contradictory, since in numberless instances the visitor could not well explain why he is present at all. But if you are to guess to what part-man you, as custodian, are to cater, the case is hopeless. If, for instance, you look upon him as a seeker of information upon some subject you specialize in, you are considering him in part, and that part, at the moment, may want nothing of your wares.

But if you make your target a whole man who seeks new experience, relaxation, adventure, imitation of friends who have told him "you mustn't miss it," curiosity, information, affirmation, and 1,000-odd other motives, you cannot fail to hit. He may be there for the explicit hope that you will reveal to him why he is there. I once remarked to a friend that we of the National Park Service are in somewhat the position of a wise waiter in a country hotel. Seeing that his guest is utterly bewildered by the bill-of-fare, the wise waiter does not directly propose a dish. He knows that the answer would be a rebellious "Don't want it." So he takes a subtle approach. "I noticed, out in the kitchen, that the chef has a very tasty stew today. It smells fine. I'm going to try it myself, when I get time to eat." Oftentimes the guest decides that this stew was exactly what he wanted, but just hadn't realized it.

Continuing the homely analogy, one thing leads to another. The guest feels comfortable after dinner. He thinks this is a pretty good hotel. Why not stay overnight? He has nothing particular to do. He takes a walk. The trees and the shrubs are greening with onleaping spring. He hasn't realized the beauty and the joy of walking for a long time. It's a better place than he thought; he is now conscious of the fact that there are a lot of interesting things to do here . . .

It is unnecessary to elaborate further. The point is that the visitor was a whole man, not merely a human mechanism looking for something to eat and then go. And a whole man has moods. If for the moment he wants nothing more, in a primitive park, than to lie under a tree and look up through the green into blue, that is part of the whole man—a temporary mood. Do not disturb him. He will be looking for something else later, and the custodians of these preservations set an ample table.

All interpreters, standing ready to serve the mood of the whole man, should cultivate humility. Not mock humility; that would be dreadful. But the true humility of one that is justly proud of his attainments, glad that it has been his fortunate lot to have a good measure of special knowledge, but infinitely patient with those who have not steered by such a constant star. It is good to remember that were you in the visitor's own bailiwick, you might be a stumbler. I am not sermonizing. I am suggesting good and understanding interpretation.

I have myself heard visitors to parks and historic monuments and museums ask some ludicrous questions. It is easy to put the visitor down as a moron. Often, however, I have been certain that these silly questions arose from a genial desire on the part of a visitor to say something so as to assure the interpreter that he was appreciative of the discourse. There not being time to consider, a stupidity resulted. Let the talk turn to something the visitor already knows: he will say nothing foolish.

Dr. Clark Wissler said, "Every ranger has the tendency to overestimate the background the tourist brings to the scene and on the other hand to underestimate the intelligence of the 'average visitor.'" I do not think this is as true today as when Dr. Wissler noted it, but adequate interpretation will not make this mistake.

Ralph Waldo Emerson wrote: "And there are patient naturalists, but they freeze their subjects under the wintry light of the understanding." Emerson had just as much admiration of the "patient naturalist" as any man. He meant simply that "the understanding" is only one of the attributes of a whole man. His natural religious spirit, his emotions, his yearning for continuity, his love of a story, his physical pleasures are among other parts of him that must be considered.

CHAPTER 7

🍃 For the Younger Mind

To the young mind everything is individual, stands by itself. . . .
Later remote things cohere and flower out from one stem.
—Ralph Waldo Emerson

Interpretation addressed to children (say, up to the age of twelve)
should not be a dilution of the presentation to adults but should
follow a fundamentally different approach. To be at its best it will
require a separate program.

Mr. Emerson was thinking, I believe, when he wrote the word "later," of a maturity of men and women when they can begin to grapple more or less successfully with abstractions. Then, indeed, "remote things flower from one stem." But Emerson would be delighted, were he here, to observe the splendid interpretive work now being done for children—the nature centers, the museum exhibits, the trail walks and talks, and all the rest—for it was not done in Emerson's day. There were the textbooks, and there was the teacher, and there were the more or less obedient pupils; and perhaps it is the best tribute to those devoted teachers to say that they were able to lay some of the educational dust that settled over the classroom where firsthand contact with the objects of study was not usually available and often not even encouraged.

If Emerson could visit an area or two of National Capital Parks, or the Cook County Forest Preserve District, or Colonial Williamsburg, Cooperstown, Old Sturbridge, or Greenfield Village—to name a few places of brilliant achievement in interpretation for children—he would agree that skillful guides are making "remote things cohere" not later, but now.

Let me give an instance. Not long ago I heard a naturalist speaking to several hundred grade-school children. In the course of his talks he used the word "ecology" several times. When I was a schoolboy we should have called that a hard word. We called any word ending in "ology" a hard word. I realize now that hard words are exactly those that represent things we are not prepared to be interested in. The naturalist had previously explained to these children that the word signified a life community of grasses and trees, of insects and birds, of rodents and reptiles, whose fortunes were bound together in their "home" place. The children were not merely interested, they were fascinated by this idea and its connotations. So the word ecology was an easy word, besides being a rather showy addition to their stock of nouns. But the point is that the concept of this association of living things, replacing a classified list of creatures all going it on their very own, is surely a coherence of remote things achieved while these children are still children.

These same children would probably complain that the words "sociology" and "theology" are hard words. They are just not yet prepared to be interested in these implications.

Considering the brilliant success of so many nature centers, museums (whether called by the name or not), and other activities of interpretation for children, I should suppose that my sixth principle will find general acceptance, considered as a principle. Naturally there will be many views as to the methods of techniques employed. It is true, too, that the most effective programs for children will, at present, be in locations most accessible for arranged visits of school groups. These are, at the present, mostly areas of day visit, though a preserve like Colonial Williamsburg is able to supply accommodations for a longer stay.

There also arises the question of cost and staffing for the maintenance of children's programs. As to this, all I would say here is that on reviewing the work now being done by the larger institutions I am sure that there is no preserve so small that it cannot employ some devices, if it desires to do interpretation at all. Few places can ever do the job as handsomely as Williamsburg, but any historic house or humble museum can use some of the basic ideas in a relatively inexpensive way.

The selection of an upper age limit of twelve years, as stated in this principle, sounds arbitrary, and is in fact so by intent. It will not be misunderstood, I am sure. Very important factors of interpretation for children continue their validity into adolescence and maturity. Reading matter, oral presentation, and other media aimed at the intermediate school level has been definitely found to interest older children and even adults.

Environmental education programs once were structured educational experiences targeted primarily to children and young adults. Today, environmental and preservation messages reach all visitors and seek to help them understand the interconnectedness of their world. (Courtesy of National Park Service)

The earliest school years find children learning the names of things at a phenomenal rate, never again matched. It is the period when we do not tire them by giving them factual information as such. The interpreter who has dealt with both young children and adults will have noted the eagerness for pure information in the one and a slight aversion to it in the other. This difference of itself suggests that interpretation for children implies a fundamentally different approach.

Surely certain characteristics of young children are carried over, with more or less diminished intensity, into the later years. One of these, of somewhat humorous aspects, is the delight in the superlative. I have followed a group of kindergarten children in a museum where some of the adventurous thrill obviously came from holding in the hand "the biggest egg" (ostrich) and "the littlest egg" (hummingbird's in nest) and from seeing the skeleton of "the biggest animal" (whale) suspended from the ceiling. There was a heroic-sized statue at one end of a room. Every child, I observed, touched this statue in passing it. I asked the interpreter-teacher why they did so. "Because it is so big. They would not have patted a statue merely life size." In a section devoted to wildfowl eggs, the attention was arrested and held by one collection of two dozen together. "It was the biggest lot," was the explanation.

Does this love of the superlative sound childlike? Yes, until you recall that several million adults spoke with great relish of the "biggest blizzard" (1888), and that other millions enjoy such superlatives as: the highest mountain in the world (Everest; though, in fact, there are several peaks in the Himalayas only a few feet less high); the biggest petrified saurian ever found; the proximity of the highest and lowest point in the United States proper (Mt. Whitney and the below-sea-level extreme in Death Valley); the first robin seen in spring; the smallest church — multiply these instances as you will.

Another characteristic very pronounced in younger children, partly because of their lack of inhibitions but carrying over in no little degree through life, is the love of personal examination through three senses other than sight and hearing. Most notable is the urge to know "what it feels like." Interpretation in the past has failed to make full use of the opportunities for satisfying this tactile urge, and at present interpretation for children is making much more use of the experi-

Never underestimate the child's great ability to see.
(Courtesy of National Park Service)

ence than is that for adults. The naturalists, perhaps, have the best chance to employ the smell and taste experiences, and some of them do it very effectively. At the door of the Little Red Schoolhouse in the Cook County Forest Preserve, I saw a small bag hanging from a nail; the label underneath read something like "Smell it. What is it?" Without a second thought I reached for it and sniffed the herb that was within. My own act was instinctive.

"What does it smell like?" It is an educational experience that goes beyond the mere odor of the object itself; it takes the child or the adult into fields of like or associated odors. An odor memory is cultivated or renewed. Children who live in rural places come to know very early by both taste and smell a large number of plant species — even the qualities of various clays — but as the country becomes more and more urbanized, there are more and more millions who can get such acquaintance and knowledge only from public preserves where interpretation is done.

Quite aside from education, the knowledge of an experience with odors is now seen as so important in the field of interpretation that when I was in Cooperstown there was a discussion of some method by which the old tavern could be given an authoritative tavern odor — a consideration that seemed to me just as important in bringing past into present as providing a historic structure with the furniture of the period. For it is part of the same aim: to give the visitor a sense of living the very experience of the ancestor.

In Cooperstown Farmers' Museum I was struck by the great number of pieces relating to rural life of the period from the Revolution to about 1850 that can be touched and handled by children and adults. Indeed, I think Dr. Louis C. Jones, the director, rather proudly told me that they had only one object that children had to be kept from, and that was because of danger of injury not to the object but to the children. Incidentally, because of this free use of touch, I wondered whether there was not considerable loss by accidental breakage or vandalism. The director said that on the contrary, such loss or repair in the previous year had been almost nil. His theory about vandalism, by the way, is worth considering. He feels that the high caliber of an exhibit, plus a warm feeling that the visitor is welcome as a guest, furnish a restraining influence. I believe that there are other considerations, but these two are certainly of high importance.

Not only are young children willing and eager to absorb a great number of factual statements as such, but we observe, once the fact is accepted, how meticulous they are that the fact should not suffer from tampering. I recall once reciting to a little three-year-old, at her request, the true-and-tried "Night before Christmas." She had heard this many times and knew it by heart. When I came to the lines "When what to my wondering eyes should appear, but a miniature sleigh and eight tiny reindeer," a spirit of mischief prompted me to say "*seven* tiny reindeer." The little lass glared at me as though I had uttered a blasphemy. She said in firm rebuke, "*Eight* tiny reindeer!" The adult would have passed it as an unimportant slip, not really caring whether Santa had eight or twelve. Perhaps this is what Emerson meant by saying that "to the young mind everything . . . stands by itself." It may also underline the necessity of patient research as a prerequisite to preparation of literature and other media for children, so that the facts will indeed be facts. However, from what I have seen of the competency of our interpreters, there is no danger from this viewpoint. More important is the truth that has been constantly impressed upon me: interpretation for children, as a branch of art, requires a very special talent.

Many writers of ability in literature for adults have failed miserably in the attempt to do books for children. I am myself a good illustration of the fact, for I once wrote a juvenile at the invitation of a publisher, the result of which effort failed to beguile even my own children, though for reasons of family loyalty they made vast pretension of being delighted. I shall leave it to others to explain precisely what this talent connotes. I have seen much of it in action and am still puzzled.

Not long ago I heard a young naturalist giving a slide talk at the newly created Rock Creek Nature Center of National Capital Parks in Washington, D.C. The old stone house formerly known as the Klingle Mansion had recently been converted into a delightful repository of exhibits and work-it-yourself devices pertaining to the natural world. There are many objects here that can be touched and handled. On this particular occasion the teachers had been invited to choose the subject. Geology, which they chose, is not an easy subject to communicate to either children or adults. But never were children more obviously given the spirit of adventure than on this occasion. Afterward I asked the naturalist if the fact that he was pretty young himself—about twenty-five—had anything to do with his success with the children. He considered, and finally said he thought not. No doubt he was right, for I have heard much older interpreters, including a college professor in his fifties, similarly adroit with child groups. Of one thing I am certain: one factor of the general talent is the ability to give the sense of companionship and conceal any show of direct instruction. Not that children resent such instruction in the classroom, but these visits to places of firsthand experience are different. Here the story becomes more important; here the adventure factor is uppermost. I suppose this is the reason why Greenfield Village has a filmstrip of previsit orientation called *A Museum Is a Story*, both to emphasize an alluring fact and also to take a supposed curse off the word "museum." Yet I doubt if children are as much frightened of that word as adults are generally supposed to be.

Albert Manucy, for many years the historian at the Castillo de San Marcos in St. Augustine, asked me, "Have you considered the ability a child possessed to identify himself with the historical scene?" Indeed I have, and among other places in Albert's own fine area. I have wondered whether this facility does not arise in the first place from the child's great ability to see. We know too well that the adult fancies he sees much when he really has seen little. Anyone who has taken a walk with a feverishly active boy of eleven years and returned limp from merely being asked to "look at that" will realize what I mean.

Now, at the Castillo de San Marcos, there used to be in the sally port a small bronze cannon pointing inward toward the parade ground. Seldom did a group of children visit the fort that one or more of them failed to ask, "What's it pointing that way for? The enemy would have come from the other direction." I never heard a similar remark from an adult. And it was usually children who showed puzzlement concerning the unmounted cannon on the fort roof: "How could they fire them?" Of course, in a matter like that we must realize that children are not usually afraid to ask questions, and many adults are, from fear of saying the wrong thing.

Further to capitalize upon this ability of the child to associate himself with the scene, some institutions are now supplying the schools with previsit material: orientation folders, descriptive literature, filmstrips on loan, and other matter designed for the intermediate grades

Children learn by listening, by doing, by touching, and by personal examination. (Courtesy of National Park Service)

or for older students, or for both. Colonial Williamsburg, which has entered this field in a large way, says that "teachers have found that students using advance briefing material have a better learning experience in Williamsburg." It could hardly be otherwise. Though such a program as Williamsburg's is expensive to maintain, I shall again point out that even small and understaffed and underendowed preserves can do *something* of the sort. I venture the statement that any museum, historic place, or other institution that attempts to bring past into present will eventually succeed or dawdle to precisely the degree it manages to interpret effectively for children. If we cannot interest with our treasures those carefree young persons whose minds are at the height of receptivity, how can we hope to interest those adults who are inevitably fogged and beset by the personal and social worries of an uneasy world?

In this chapter I have attempted to do little more than to give personal observations of interpretation for children that seemed to support the view that the principle involved is truly a principle, and that it is being most effectively activated by many institutions and by interpreters. Nothing that I have noted should be taken as hinting that I have proficiency in child psychology, which indeed I have not. I reiterate that I am convinced that interpretation for children requires a very special aptitude, though this does not mean that certain persons may not have talent to conduct programs for both children and adults, or even for those most difficult visitors, the adolescents, who have in the past few years been marked and treated—as I believe most unfairly—as being almost a distinct species of the genus Homo.

Also, I should add that though I have mentioned but a few of the admirable programs currently conducted, I have chosen these with no thought of being discriminatory. All around us amazingly fine work in interpretation for children is going on. Besides, my reports of institutions that I have not been able to visit, and my accumulation of their bulletins, brochures, quiz sheets, and the like, have been vastly encouraging. Finally, to applaud the rapid increase and the excellence of this effort is not to depreciate the constant improvement of interpretation aimed at the adult.

Part II

CHAPTER 8

The Written Word

A spade is not sharpened by being called a geotome.
—*Norman D. Newell*

This chapter does not offer a course in the writing of interpretive signs, markers, labels, or printed literature. It presents thoughts and examples consonant with the principles stated in the first part of the book.

I feel sure that someday there will be a school with regular sessions held successively in at least four regions of the United States, where those of the National Park Service, and members of other agencies concerned with the graphic phases of interpretation, will meet to compare experiences, discuss examples, present their own productions for discussion and assay, and listen to at least one talk by a selected person who has made notable progress in this difficult field of expression. Whoever gives this talk will certainly be one who sincerely admits that he himself is still a patient student. The intricacies of this branch of art make it certain that no one person will ever be its complete master.

To begin a little discursively, I will note the fact that many years ago, being enamored of the challenge of interpretation, I set myself the task of collecting and studying what we may refer to as the "inscription." This specifically includes relatively brief messages, indoors or without, aiming at something deeper than mere information.

I began with Greek epigraphy. I confess that I never reaped any great harvest there, for the Greek inscription was primarily, by intent, a tiny jewel of poetry, even when comic. One thing, however, makes this ancient artistic form worth our attention: the success in making a few words tell a full and moving story. The celebrated epigram of Simonides (any English translation can but feebly capture its original elegance) engraved on a monument at Thermopylae is worth mentioning:

Go tell the Spartans, thou that passest by,
That here, obedient to their laws, we lie.

The couplet expressed to the Greek wayfarer as much as pages of history text could have. No wonder he wept when he read it.

One more quotation from classical inscription will suffice. If you happened to know that St. Paul's Cathedral in London was designed by Sir Christopher Wren, you would naturally expect to see there either a blunt announcement of that fact or a statue of the architect. What you see is a laconic inscription: "Si monumentum requiris, circumspice." (If it is my memorial you are looking for, gaze around you.)

A tablet of 500 words recounting the achievements of Wren would be feeble compared with that understatement.

First, we should consider what place inscriptions of the several kinds occupy in the scheme of the interpretation of an area. That they constitute a rock bottom there can be no doubt. Some millions of visitors are going to receive their first—and many will unfortunately get their only—impressions from this source. Especially in an area set aside for its scientific values, a sign employing technical and unfamiliar language may serve to chill the interest in the whole. If he cannot readily understand the interpretive sign or label, the visitor may easily conclude that the place is a little beyond his normal capacity to enjoy.

A directional sign may be scrawled with red chalk on a shingle and prove to be better than none: it serves to give information that is of first importance. This is not true with the interpretive marker. I have noted many cases where a blundering marker was worse than nothing at all. Consider this one, not actually used, but suggested for a spot near the salt pools in Death Valley. It begins: "The remnant of ancient ice-age Lake Manly maintains its water level from 4 to several feet beneath the uppermost salt layers . . ."

What is the visitor unskilled in geology—particularly the regional geology—to think of that? This sign accosts him with the ice age, of which he certainly has only the vaguest notion, and with Lake Manly, nonexistent now except underneath the salt, of which he cannot be expected to know anything. Death Valley is said to be the "paradise of

Wayside exhibits help interpret features in plain sight of visitors. Text explaining the feature promotes revelation based on information. (Photo by R. Bruce Craig)

the geologist." It can be the wonderland of the nongeologist, too, but not if you start with an introduction like that.

I recall a case of objects in a museum in the South, where war materials of the Civil War period are displayed. The label refers to the pistols and other objects as "artifacts." Truly, since they were made by man, they are artifacts. But they are relics, aren't they? Isn't that what we commonly call them? Why call them by a name that makes the visitor think he is facing something obscure?

Such examples as these take us directly to what I shall now discuss, which is the frame of mind and the basic considerations from which a good inscription must spring. The creation of the written interpretive work—and it is equally true, of course, of the preparation of oral material—is a matter of two stages: thinking and composition. Of these two, it must be apparent that the first is the more important. If the thinking is sound and the composition halting, the result will never be entirely bad. On the other hand, if the thinking is poor, even if the writing is brilliant, the result is worthless or even mischievous. Except for the rare instances of inspiration, I should guess that the adequate interpretive inscription will be the result of 90 percent thinking and 10 percent composition. Inspiration is usually the mirrored reflection of hard work.

THINKING

Probably the most common error in creating interpretive matter of all kinds derives from the fact that the writer has in mind the question: "What is it I wish to say?" It is of no importance whatever, as yet, what I wish to say. I have not reached that point. The important thing is: What would the prospective reader wish to read? And what can I say in brief, inspiring, and luring terms about this area in language that he will readily comprehend?

For myself, I have found in the writing of inscriptions that it is of great advantage to have in mind some person of my acquaintance and write straight to him. In the days when I was doing much public speaking, I found it useful (and other speakers have told me the same thing) to pick out some cheerful inviting countenance in the audience and mainly direct my words to her or to him. It develops a conversational as opposed to a starched-shirt manner.

It seems hardly necessary to say that the preliminary thinking is dominated by a love of the subject in hand, plus an active interest in people. Axiom: whatever is written without enthusiasm will be read without interest.

It is highly necessary to visualize the encounter between your message and the visitors. It is useful to the writer to be familiar with the exact spot where the inscription will be placed, but this is not absolutely necessary. Again, it is a great help if one can know of certain spots where almost invariably the visitors ask one leading question, as at Badwater, in Death Valley.

But more important is to have answered for yourself, as interpreter, the vital questions: "What is the keynote of this whole place? What is the overall reason why it should have been preserved?" It is for this reason that I have in time past suggested what I call the "master-marker" that would be, as one might say, the title of the book, and the rest of the markers would be chapter heads. Not every area would lend itself to this scheme; in some the master-marker would be the only marker. As to where such a master-marker would be placed, the administrator of the area should best know. In some cases, headquarters would be the favorable location; in others, the place of largest congregation. But certainly neither the master-marker, nor indeed any inscription, should intrude itself between visitor and the object intended to delight and impress. And there are spots where no interpretive sign should be erected. Nature, and even artifice, can sometimes speak for itself better than the interpreter can. Personally, I should not ever wish to see a marker exactly upon the bald summit of Cadillac, in Acadia National Park.

Sometimes a quotation will be found more effective than anything we can currently invent, to project the right mood into the mind of a reader. The Minute-Man inscription on the boulder at Lexington Green may be taken as an example:

Line of the Minute-Men
April 19, 1775
Stand Your Ground
Don't Fire unless Fired Upon
But if They Mean to Have a War
Let it Begin Here
—Captain Parker

Can you imagine anything we can now say of the outbreak of the Revolutionary War that would be better than this?

Or, at the lovely Brookgreen Gardens in South Carolina, where the Huntingtons established and endowed the largest outdoor museum of sculpture in the world, in the shade of the live oaks you are greeted with this quotation from the canticle of St. Francis of Assisi:

Praised be thou, my Lord, with all thy creatures,
Especially the honored Brother Sun,
Who makes the day and illumines us through thee.
And he is beautiful and radiant with great splendor;
Bears the signification of thee, Most High One.

In reading a life of Alexander von Humbolt recently, I came upon a quotation that might be effectively used in these days of fear and frustration: "Let those who are wearied with the clash of warring nations . . . turn their attention to the silent life of vegetation . . . and remember that the earth continues to teem with new life."

That sentence heartened me, somehow, and I feel sure that if I had stumbled upon it in one of our many quiet woodland or meadow retreats I should have thrown back my shoulders and taken on a touch of renewed confidence. So, as interpreter I ask myself, "Why should not others get the same result, since I am just one of the crowd?"

Still, as to quotations, we must consider that in spite of the fact that thousands of fine things have been said, worthy of preservation in print, it is really uncommon to find one that exactly fits the needs we are discussing. And of course it is only too human, when one is stymied in the sweating-out of a good sign, to seek a quotation as the easy way out.

One of the choicest signs I know is that by Bob Mann, in the Forest Preserve District of Cook County, Illinois:

I am an Old Time Country Lane
Now I have been
Officially Vacated and Closed
(I never liked automobiles anyway)
I invite you to walk—as folks
have walked for generations

and be friendly with my trees
my flowers and my wild creatures.

What an invitation that sign is to the tired, restless, perplexed, and jaded soul! Bob wrote to me humorously that the sign was composed "mit beer." I don't care whether it was dashed off on the spur of the moment, or laboriously wrought. What I do know—and we are talking at this moment not of composition but of thinking—is that it could not have been born of anything but years of sheer affection for and understanding of nature and people, and the needs of people.

Perhaps this brief comment will serve to point out the indispensability of deep meditation of all the conditions to be met, of the subject and of people and their limitations, before any writing whatever is attempted. I suppose it sums up this way: you must be in love with your material, and you must be in tune with your fellow man. What ensues is composition; not easy, needing pitiless editing and cool criticism, full of pitfalls, barbed with discouraging false starts and notes—but a great joy when the bull's-eye is hit. But the thinking will determine the result.

COMPOSITION

The chief thing that makes the wording of good inscriptions so exacting is the requirement of brevity. "Anybody can write a novel," said a famous magazine editor to me one day, "but there are few good short-story writers." While this was a deliberate exaggeration, for not everyone *can* write an acceptable novel, the statement was based upon an important truth.

Interpretive signs, museum labels, and the like will be usually read by standing people. There are exceptions, such as when a drive-off permits people to remain in an automobile and read. People are not conditioned, save perhaps for straphanging commuters, to much reading while standing. I found in Blue Ridge Parkway, at the entrance to a self-guiding trail, a large glass-covered case that contained, in hand-lettered capital letters, several hundred words of the best writing I had seen in a long time. It was salty, neatly turned, with the homeliness of the mountains and mountain people. It delighted me. But I observed that visitors merely gave it a glance and turned away. It was too long, and it was in capital letters. Except for headlines, readers are not conditioned to "caps." They read them under eye protest.

Brevity, of course, is to be taken comparatively. What would be sufficiently laconic in one circumstance would be too long in another. Generally speaking, an area of day visitation will require briefer inscriptions than one where people feel a greater sense of leisure. I concluded after a stay in Death Valley that interpretive signs could be somewhat longer there (if the subject so indicated) than in most of the park system areas.

Three kinds of brevity defeat their purpose. One is the sort called telegraphic, where articles "a" and "the" and even words are omitted. I have just looked at an expensively executed bronze plaque, otherwise satisfactory, which was ruined by this bad writing and bad taste. Another is the kind where, in striving for brevity, the sign fails to convey an adequate message. Much as we desire to avoid unnecessary wordage, reasonable latitude in length must be allowed. The third case is really an error in preliminary thinking, rather than in composition. A sign may include a statement that requires an explanation, but for brevity's sake the explanation is omitted. An illustration of this I saw at Montezuma Castle. A sign there says that "Montezuma is a misnomer." ("Misnomer" is a fancy word for "wrongly named." It is not in common use.) It is true that Montezuma the Aztec had nothing to do with this area, but you here read something that is meaningless unless explained. The answer probably is that it need not have been mentioned at all. It is the sort of information that may well fit into a folder or handbook, where it can be properly handled.

Ronald Lee handed me this inscription, which he saw in the Southwest:

A Building Stood Here Before 1680.
It was Wrecked in
The Great Indian Uprising.
This House Incorporates
What Remains.

This is brief, and I judge from what I know of the building, entirely adequate.

Here is an example of a brevity that makes for inertness and fail-

ure to capture interest, when the addition of a few words would create an interesting mental picture:

This Rock
Marks the Spot
Where
Daniel Webster
Spoke
To About 15000 People
at
The Whig Convention
July 7 and 8 1840
Erected by the Stratton Mountain Club

It was not a convention in the present political-party sense, but
that is not the serious error in the inscription. The point is that the
sign is dead when it could be very much alive, for this political rally
of 1840 was actually an amazing thing. Let us see if we can make it
move. Daniel Webster began his speech on this occasion with the
words: "From above the clouds, I address you . . ." So, as his opening
words create at once the picture of a great crowd being on a high
mountain, why not begin with the quotation?

"From Above the Clouds I Address You . . ."
Daniel Webster
Statesman and Orator
Spoke Here
to 15000 people
Who had Come in Farm Wagons
In Carriages
and Afoot
To the Rally
For "Tippecanoe" Harrison
For President
in July 1840.

Aside from the fact that few persons now know what a Whig was,
while most people have heard of William Henry Harrison, the inscription now has movement. It was no small thing for 15,000 people

to toil up a high mountain to hear oratory. They took their politics seriously in those days.

Wherever this element of movement in a sign is possible, it is most effective. Here is a sample from the New Hampshire State Preserve at Franconia Notch:

> The Basin
> Over a period of centuries
> a pothole was formed by the
> action of a large stone
> *turning* and *spinning*
> under the pressure of *rushing*
> *whirling* water, in a depression
> of the granite stream-bed.

The italics in the above are of course mine. They are legitimate words that graphically describe how the pothole was formed, and I do not think the use of four participles for this purpose was over-doing it.

Movement may be suggested by a picture. On U.S. Route 14 through Ure Pass at Divide there is a sign: "Yonder is Cripple Creek." Underneath is a miner with his burro, and under that: "World's Greatest Gold Camp." The picture furnishes the sense of motion.

HUMOR

We now arrive at one of the touchiest qualities of inscriptional writing—humor. At the outset we can all agree that its use should be with discretion, finesse, and fitness. Humor out of place is a sad excrescence. Humor in harmony with the thing, and the mood, is a charm to most people. What is humor? Thackery thought it was "a mixture of love and wit." Wit alone is often biting and unkind. Humor, especially that of the turn of phrase, or the oddity of conceit, brings a contented smile. In Bob Mann's old-time country lane sign, the line "I never liked automobiles anyway" is a flash of humor. Bob makes the old lane speak its mind and gives it a personality.

The Montana highway signs that have cheered everyone who has driven the roads of that state have many touches of true humor. They thus distinguish these inscriptions and earn a national comment. In the old days, says one of these signs, "you rode a saddle horse to get places. Some people wish it were still like that." Here is a nice dab of the nostalgic that appeals to us all; for enmeshed as we are in the mechanical web, we all yearn for an hour with mud pies and oxen.

"There are people," said Emerson in an essay on "Culture," "who can never understand a trope, or any second or expanded sense given to your words, or any humor; but remain literalists after hearing music and poetry and rhetoric and wit, of seventy years. They are past the help of surgeon or clergy."

You think of Emerson as a learned philosopher and hardly expect to hear him say anything funny. Nor does he say anything *funny*. But if there is any more delicate sally of humor that makes you bubble joyously in your inwards than the paragraph about the pale scholar with bent brow and firm intent, who goes out into his garden to get "a juster statement of his thought," finds himself pulling weeds, and ends by being "duped by a dandelion"—I know not where to find it. (Essay on "Wealth.")

Inscriptional matter should be written generally with lightness but never with levity. Get that clear distinction in your mind, and you save yourself from what is slangily called the corny. It is the light touch that brings the sunshine out of the cloud. As an example I present an inscription on a monument at Quebec, honoring both France's general Montcalm and Britain's general Wolfe: "Valor gave them a common death, history a common fame and posterity a common monument."

Here is a noble subject, nobly approached; but observe that unlike many a heavy-handed and lugubrious treatment, it has the lightness of touch that, in this case, happens to be part of the genius of the French tongue (this quotation being a translation). I admit that this whole subject is a difficult one. It is one of those things about language that either you feel or you do not. If you do not see the shades of difference between the heavy and the light attack, you are not as yet equipped to write inscriptional matter.

I suggest the following inscription for some desert spot, where a welcome *remada* is surrounded by desert plants. There is no warrant herein for the slightest humor. We wish to tell a story and give a warning. But the touch is light:

The desert is a severe mother, bent more on justice than on mercy. Through generations of survival these plants around you have found means of protecting themselves from death by heat and drouth. Note the varied ways. You, too, must learn the wisdom of the desert if you would be safe within it.

When you are able to write with a light touch, without indulging in humor, then you shall be permitted to write humor with a light touch. That, to me, sums up the matter.

CHAPTER 9 ❧ Past into Present

He held it always as a maxim, that History did greatly serve . . . to the ordering of a man's life. For he counted it as, in certain ways, more effectual than Philosophy, which indeed instructs men with words; but History thrills them with examples and makes them partakers of things and times which are past. —*Gassendi*, Life of Peiresc

Although none of the wilderness preserves are without some historical associations, this chapter will primarily concern itself with the prehistoric and historic areas of the National Park System, and of the many other shrines, publicly and privately owned and administered, where the effort is made by interpreters to turn back the pages of time and establish a vital relationship between the visitor and the memorialized people and events.

As to the primitive parks, however, this much may be said: that of all the millions of visitors to them, the fullest appreciation of unspoiled nature is found by those who are willing to imitate in some degree the experiences of the pioneers, even though it be actually a pale partaking, devoid of most of the hardships and dangers. Campers, certainly rather than cruisers of the roads; yet only those campers who are willing to leave the spots of congregation and strike into the back country may be said truly to participate. We shall look closely at this rather baffling word "participate" in the following pages. Even if the valiant few who taste the joys of absolute self-reliant freedom of the wilderness are not condemned to live off the land as the mountain men and French voyageurs did, they return home with a keen perception of the rigors that faced the pioneer.

Visiting the places that have been made famous and treasurable by the acts of men and women, where the story is told of courage and self-sacrifice, of dauntless patriotism, of statesmanship and inventive genius, of folkways, of husbandry or of the clash of armed men following their ideals to the valley of the shadow—all this offers a very different kind of experience. These places may be physically beautiful, and they may exemplify artisanship of the highest order, and furnishings of the most exquisite taste; but whether they are those things, or whether they are humble log cabins, rudely equipped, in a bleak environment, they all point to the same thing—they represent the life and acts of people. Consequently, the interpreter will endeavor, if he is presenting a historic house, to "people" that house. Architecture and furnishings are much; we admire and draw conclusions from them, but we must find the art to keep them from seeming to have been frozen at a moment of time when nobody was at home.

The prehistoric ruin must somehow manage to convey the notion to the visitor that the ancients who lived there might come back this very night and renew possession, and that there will be a renewal of the grinding of corn, the cries of children, and the making of love and feasting. This must not be taken too literally. I am trying to project a possible feeling. The battlefield of our great fratricidal American war is not merely a place of strategy and tactics; not a place where regiments moved this way and that like checkers on the board; not merely a spot where something was decided that would lead to another decision. It is a place of the thoughts and acts of men, of their ideals and memories; a place where on the evening of a fatal tomorrow men could joke and sing; a place of people, not armies. For we Americans are not descendants of a regiment; we are sprung from men and women.

If you go into that charming Adams house in Quincy, Massachusetts, you see a house that was occupied by several generations of one of our most extraordinary families—rugged individualists, if there ever were any; intellectuals, unspectacular, nonconformists. In Oregon is the home of John McLoughlin, "father of the Oregon Territory," another rugged individualist, but how different from the Adamses! At Hyde Park there are the homes of Frederick Vanderbilt and Franklin D. Roosevelt, each representing a sharply etched way of life in a period of our history. But wherever, and whatever, in the places devoted to human history the objective of interpretation remains unchanged: to bring to the eye and understanding of the visitor not just a house, a ruin, or a battlefield, but a house of living people, a prehistoric ruin of real folks, a battlefield where men were only incidentally—even if importantly—in uniform. I was thrilled once at the sight of a picture of a poor ragged fragment of a defeated Confederate band, straggling past an officer standing on a hillock by the side of the road, and bravely managing a salute out of their remaining morale. Hardly a whole uniform among them! I said to myself, "*This was the war*."

I shall not elaborate further on this. All understanding interpreters know as well as I what the ideal interpretation implies: re-creation of the past, and kinship with it. The problem is how to achieve this desirable end. It is not easy. It is quite the contrary. There are hundreds of physical difficulties in the way of letting the visitor and the thing indulge in a desirable intimacy. Objects are often fragile, and many structures cannot bear indiscriminate use. The vandal is dreaded. There are many irreplaceable treasures. No generalization as to management will hold, for what could be tolerated or encouraged in one place would be speedily fatal to another. So, in interpretive effort we are constantly considering ways and means of bringing the past to the present, for the stimulation of our visitors, as local conditions may permit. Two of the devices frequently discussed in the field of interpretation are demonstration and participation. We shall look at those, and it may be that we can add a third.

DEMONSTRATION

Dr. John Merriam once quoted with great relish a characteristic instance in the Middle Ages of depending upon theory and description, when a simple demonstration would have resolved all difficulties at once. There was a spirited discussion among a group of scientific men over the nature and number of teeth possessed by a horse. Literature was quoted, authority was marshalled, and the discussion was raging ineffectively when somebody abruptly suggested that they go out and get a horse.

Demonstration is the act of "bringing in the horse." You may write pages or talk interminably to me about the process of grinding flour and meal between stones revolved by a wheel driven by the flow of a stream, and I shall still be too little aware of what actually takes place. After seeing the operation in process at Mabry's Mill on the Blue Ridge Parkway, at Rock Creek Park in Washington, D.C., or at Spring Mill State Park in Indiana, my curiosity is satisfied. We must remember that our country has become so greatly urbanized that there are now millions of adults and children who have never seen a cow milked.

Living history programs sometimes include interpretive demonstrations. (Photo by R. Bruce Craig)

The Steel Institute has reconstructed, on its original site and in the most faithful replica, the first successful ironworks in America. On the Saugus River in Massachusetts, at stated intervals (because the water must be used sparingly) the visitor may see not merely the physical equipment and structures, but the movement of the machinery of the rolling and slitting mill. At the fine Farmers' Museum at Cooperstown, thousands of delighted visitors watch the old-time process of breaking flax, of weaving, and of candle making; and to make the demonstration even more impressive, a little plot of soil shows, nearby, flax plants in growth.

On the top of the Castillo de San Marcos in St. Augustine, the visitor sees some ancient cannon, lying on the roof with muzzles pointing ineffectively through the ports. It is obvious that something is missing in the picture. It is necessary to explain that these supine implements, in their present position, could not be used at all. When I was last at the fine old Spanish fort, the superintendent was trying to get funds that would mount a few such guns on carriages, with the necessary equipment to demonstrate how they were actually used. A demonstration, most illuminating, could show the whole procedure up to the moment of actual firing.

Again, at this Castillo de San Marcos, there is a provocative instance of how demonstration can be turned into participation, and thus obtain both elements at once. For many years the guides at the fort have paused at the doorway of one of its storerooms, which in the early Spanish days was secured by an ingenious three-way lock. The leader of the tour never failed to interest his group when he demonstrated exactly how the locking-up was done. One day an experiment was tried. After his demonstration the ranger invited one of his group, "Come and do it yourself." The effect was clearly stimulating. Though the participation was immediately that of only one person, the rest of the group somehow felt that *they* were helping to do it. An unexpected by-product of this simple expedient was told to me by one of the guides. He said, "That demonstration at the doorway seems also to have the effect of pulling my group closer to me all the rest of the tour."

One of the most ingenious devices of demonstration I have seen was in the Desert Museum in Phoenix, Arizona. The peculiar methods by which desert plants resist the terrific dehydration of the torrid summers are familiar matters of descriptive talks and literature. But, choosing the great saguaro cactus as an example, some good thinking in interpretation has partly exposed the root system of a living plant and affixed a thermometer that demonstrated how the plant keeps its internal temperature constantly below the heat of the air. This is most effective demonstration, and while it seems of a very special kind and opportunity, I have not the least doubt that we could find in our primitive areas many related chances.

Once, in Big Bend National Park, I had Natt Dodge take for me a color slide of a Mexican laborer standing in a clump of lechuguilla plants. Over his shoulder is carried a bag of the sort the natives have for centuries woven (as well as ropes, bridles, and dozens of other things) from this very plant. Among our most effective efforts at interpretation are the demonstrations of how not only aboriginal people but our own pioneers used the material that they found at hand to create the things they had to have. A demonstration of the actual processing of the lechuguilla would have been, of course, even better; but that, like so many other opportunities that must be reluctantly passed up, meets administrative difficulties.

I could go from here to a long list of excellent demonstrations that are actually being done either in National Park Service areas or by other interpretive agencies, but the point I wish to make is that we have by no means more than skimmed the surface of the possibilities in demonstration. That demonstrations will never be sufficiently numerous in any place of interpretation I sadly admit. No doubt local peculiarities often forbid them. It must be added, too, that lack of money and personnel have prevented, in the past, such desirable development of this fruitful educational device. Still, I am persuaded that in many areas much can be done with little, if imaginative and deliberate assessment of the possibilities is employed.

Finally, the word "demonstration" and its implication are readily understood by all those engaged in interpretation. It would be fine if we could say as much of the commonly used partner word:

PARTICIPATION

Here is another term in interpretation that, like the very word "interpretation" itself, needs a reasonably well-accepted definition. I say reasonably, because it has already become clear to me that we interpreters are never going to agree precisely upon the point where "participation" begins to be of sufficient weight to merit the term. What we can all agree upon without reservation is that the thing we mean by the word is of the utmost importance in enlivening the visitor's sense of, and feeling for, the past in natural and human history. To argue about the definition of the word is farthest from my purpose. My feeling simply is that we should have, when we use any word, a fairly general tacit acceptance.

The dictionary will not help you. It is another of those words to which interpretive activities have given a special significance. The only thing that will help is the discussion of examples, ranging from what we all, without dissent, admit as participation, through examples that will be disputed, and finally down to instances where most of us will feel that the word ceases to have any significance at all.

To me, it is elementary that participation, in our sphere of interpretation, must be physical. When you try to make it include what is wholly or predominantly mental, the word is stretched beyond meaning. Not only must it imply a physical act, it must also be something that the participant himself would regard as, for him, novel, special, and important. I cannot believe that a man who eats hasty pudding and codfish balls really thinks that he is participating in the life of the provincial Boston of Cotton Mather; on the other hand, I am quite sure that when he takes the barge ride on the old C&O Canal, in our National Capital Parks, he feels the distinct pleasure of reverting to a period that has long gone. He sees the mules tugging at the towrope, and passing through the locks can easily imagine himself a traveler to Cumberland, taking his ease on deck and greeting his neighbors at the halting places.

On the contrary, the group headed by a Supreme Court justice that walked the C&O Canal a few years ago were not participating. It was a good and amusing stunt, but the canal was a means of common carriage in its heyday, and about the only pedestrians were the mule skinners.

The carriage rides at Colonial Williamsburg, as I see it, come gracefully within the meaning of our term. Yet these have not quite the degree of true participation that John D. Rockefeller Jr., with fine imagination, planned for Acadia National Park when he created the carriage roads that were to give a taste of the horse-and-buggy days and a leisurely savouring of the joys of driving a lovely countryside, with ample opportunity of viewing unspoiled natural scenes. Alas! The horse became too nearly extinct, and liveries too expensive, before the plan could ripen its humane fruit.

Nobody would question a high degree of true participation in the days when visitors could climb the ladders to the cliff dwellings at Montezuma Castle in Arizona, a vivid experience that had to be written off when it became clear that the fragile ruins could not endure the heavy visitation. But the rutted roadways over which the pioneers of the Oregon migration passed are still available, and so are the by-passed stretches of trail that diverge at many points from the parkway of the Natchez Trace. At Pipestone National Monument I suppose it would be possible to obtain a pipe of the identical catlinite from which for centuries the Indians made their calumets. The pipe could be filled with the "kinnikinnick" or inner bark of the dogwood that still grows abundantly, thus affording anyone, with the curiosity to do it, the identical material for true participation.

I was at Death Valley National Monument one day, gazing at the famous well of the Bennett-Arcane party of 1849, when a family arrived at the spot in an automobile. One of the party, a girl of about fifteen, came over to the pool with a tin cup, leaned as far out as possible, scooped up some of the water and drank it with gusto. I had the impression, though she did not say so, that it was a deliberate act of participation on her part. At any rate, I so considered it.

Not because of any close relationship to the participation offered in our areas, but because it seems to me to point to an acme of true participation from which we can determine the validity of various shades of meaning of the word, I include here an experience mentioned in a current scientific magazine. Two Danish archaeologists, curious about the aboriginal use of the stone axe in felling trees, as well as the subsequent burning and planting of such a cleared area (the primitive practice in agriculture), engaged in a well-studied experiment. Using artifacts that had been dug from a swamp, they actually felled large trees, and burned and cleared and planted. They discovered exactly how the chopping was done, for they found that a stone axe freely swung, as we use a steel implement, broke or chipped under the force of the blow, whereas a short, pecking stroke did the work and did not injure the tool. Without describing this experiment further, it occurs to me that it was a classic of participation from beginning to end. (If you had been watching them in the course of their work, for you it would have been a demonstration.)

Visitors to our archaeological areas would be certainly participating if they were to take a handful of corn grains and with mano and metate grind this corn to meal. I should like to see this opportunity generally afforded to the visitor. He would not necessarily have to use the ancient artifacts, for the Mexicans are currently manufacturing plenty of contemporary manos and metates for their own use. But I also know that these artifacts exist in great abundance all over the Southwest, and it would take several centuries to use up the supply.

All in all, the opportunities for bringing to the visitor a journey into the past by means of participation will never be as abundant as we should like. The point I make is that participation and demonstration are such priceless ingredients of interpretation that we should diligently search for possibilities and never let slip a real opportunity for including them.

But there is another effective implement of interpretation that is clearly neither demonstration nor participation. I shall call it:

ANIMATION

If you do not happen to like the word "animation," perhaps you will prefer to call it "local color" or "atmosphere." I like the word animation to describe the thing, because to animate is to give life, to vivify. Again, the definition is not so important if we can agree on what the activity is, or can be.

On a Sunday afternoon I went to the Custis-Lee Mansion, "Arlington House," just across the Potomac River from Washington, D.C. As I entered, somebody was playing the piano. It seemed so perfectly natural that somebody would be playing a piano in a house that had sheltered the Custises and the Lees, or indeed in any historic house where people had lived! I had been many times in this famous home and had delighted in its beautiful maintenance. I had, in truth, never actually felt it to be cold; but like so many other precious relics of the past, its treasures have to be safeguarded, and most of the rooms can be seen only from their doorways. That is a penalty we must pay for preservation.

The homes of great leaders such as Thomas Jefferson's Monticello not only enable the interpreter to tell the story of a Founding Father but also the social history of times past. (Photo by R. Bruce Craig)

But now, I felt that this house was peopled. Not by visitors like my-self, but by those who had best right there—the men and women who loved the place because it was home. In a drawing room an attractive girl, costumed in the period of 1860, was playing the very tunes that were current at that time. It could have been a neighbor lass of Miss Mary Custis at the instrument, which itself was of the very period. There was nothing obtrusive about the music, and I noted with plea-sure that most of the visitors were not curious about it, a sure sign that it was in perfect harmony and accepted as part of the re-creation.

On one occasion there was a "St. Patrick's Day Celebration" at Arlington House. Now that is not in harmony, someone might say. But if they did so say, they would be ignorant of the fact that George Washington Parke Custis was noted for his sympathy with the Irish cause of freedom, in that day when it was a burning political ques-tion. He wrote an ode to "Young Ireland," gave many addresses on the subject, and threw himself into the ardent dispute with all his accustomed vigor. It *was* in harmony, this celebration, and it helped to people that mansion. It was animation.

I believe that many of the beautifully planned and executed de-vices at Colonial Williamsburg, aimed at bringing past into present for visitors, can properly be described as animation. But whether or not we wish to call them so, we should realize that effective opportu-nities for such interpretation lie all around us in our activities.

An enduring sense of the heritage from our fathers is vital to the future, and this knowledge is to be gained by keeping the past a living reality. *There* is strength. I remember talking one day with Ronald Lee about the pleasant feeling of participation I had had in walking por-tions of the old Oregon Trail in western Nebraska and Wyoming. "But it is more than that," said Ronnie, speaking for himself as a west-erner. "To me it brings a sharp realization that the West is a part of our great Whole, and has its share in the general heritage. It gives us the thrill that we belong."

One of my favorite books is John Merriam's *The Living Past*.* His title alone supplies us with an interpretative ideal.

* The experience described by Merriam at Canyon de Chelly, page 37 of the 1930 edition, seems to me an ideal example of what I mean by anima-tion.

CHAPTER 10 🔥 Nothing in Excess

Too much noise deafens us; too much light dazzles us; too much distance or too much proximity impedes vision; too much length or too much brevity of discourse obscures it; too much truth astonishes* us.
—*Blaise Pascal*

The saying "nothing in excess" is attributed to several of the Greek "wise men," but in truth it is far older than that. It probably dates from the time when a primitive man tried to bolt too large a hunk of mammoth meat.

For myself I got a taste of this wholesome injunction years ago when I had a country house that needed wooden shingles. I hired an old cunning carpenter of the neighborhood to do the job, but then I was seized with the ambition to try my own hand at laying a square. The experienced eyes watched me for a few moments. Then he said, "Would ye take a little advice? The way you're doing, you'll split the shingles. Never give the nail *that last tap*."

Whenever I am visiting one of our preserved areas, whether a park or a museum or a historic house, and whenever I hear an oral interpretation or read a written one, I am sometimes reminded of that homely remark. There are so many instances where, injuriously and to the detriment of an otherwise fine presentation, the nail has been given "that last tap." The descriptive folder that does not end when enough has been said; the last twenty color slides that collapse the camel; the "one more last thought" of an earnest speaker who bulges with an enthusiasm wholly laudable; the museum that responds to the humane thought "we just can't leave that out"—all these excesses spring from admirable intentions. But the interpreter must survey his work from the point of view of the visitor and take into consideration all the factors that make an audience restive, easily sidetracked, and too readily gorged, especially when it has little familiarity with the subject.

* Astonish, in the old sense of "bewilder."

I recall one rather comic instance of the "last tap" in a certain museum filled with a display of highly specialized objects brought together by a manufacturer of fine cultural leanings. The museum is beautifully housed, free to the public, and is of such importance that the school authorities of the city make a visit to it a prescription for the children at some time during their study years.

Unfortunately, almost the very first thing the young visitors observe when they enter the first hall is a painting. The picture, to be sure, is by one of the old masters, and very fine. Nor is the subject alien to the objects on display. The difficulty is that the principal figure in the painting is a lady who, at the moment the artist saw her, was not wearing any clothes. She is very lovely, and there is no tinge of vulgarity in the art. But children are children, and high school pupils are adolescents, and the day I happened to be in the museum, a troop of young irrepressibles was gathered around the picture poking each other in the ribs and giggling. From that moment, the excellent exhibit was in grave danger of disappearing down the drain, speaking from the standpoint of education.

The answer is simple. The owner of the painting considered it fine art, and it is; he felt that it could be displayed with propriety, and it can; he was sure that it fitted with the general subject of the museum, and he was right; but he could not bear to leave it out, and he was wrong. It is excess. The display would be better off without it.

In Lafayette Square, in Washington, D.C., there is a statue of Thaddeus Kosciusko, the famed Polish military engineer who fought for American independence. Well he deserved a memorial in the capital city of the nation. But the base of the statue bears the inscription, "Freedom shrieked as Kosciusko fell." Of course, freedom did nothing of the sort. Freedom never shrieks, however much it may honor, esteem, or lament. It may be said that the quotation is from a poem of Thomas Campbell, "The Pleasures of Hope." In a whole poem and regarded as a bit of license, it may pass. But in an inscription it can be seen only as an error of excess. Inscriptions, particularly when dealing with noble subjects, should avoid words that produce undignified pictures.

In interpretive markers we should be chary of using words like "heroes." Certainly the men were heroes who are so described; but it is better to tell what they did, and the visitor will not forget that the acts were heroic. Indeed, when it occurs to him that it was hero-ism, it is borne in upon him more forcefully than if he were told so. "They fought against great odds, but they held their position." This sentence proves they were valiant, without using the word.

I say in another chapter that you do not make a scene more beau-tiful by calling it beautiful. In a sense, you make it a little less so. It is the same with excessive words. Let us cultivate the power that lies in understatement.

I find in my notes the following reference in quotes: "that admi-rable restraint which springs from good taste and perfect under-standing of the limitations of the subject." I do not know now whether I wrote this or whether I copied it somewhere. Anyway, it is to the point. Such poise is an indication that the interpreter feels deeply and thinks clearly about the essence of what he has in his custody.

Let us not fall into the humorous mistake of the florid exponent of "chamber of commerce" literature. It is self-defeating when issued to persons of judgment. If you tell me that your locality combines the grandeur of the Alps with the serenity of an English village, and the historical pageant of the Loire Valley with the mystery of Tibet, I reply that there is no such damned place, and if there were, I should avoid it; and I drop your folder into the wastebasket.

There are so many and such varied pitfalls in this matter of excess that I can here give but a hint of the general danger. Even this much I dislike to do, since I have planned the book almost wholly upon the side of affirmation and construction; but the devil is always at our elbow, suggesting that one last touch of virtuosity. When in doubt, say "no." The world has never been much hurt by abstentions.

"Multiplication is vexation," the children of the McGuffey Reader period used to chant; and so it is, in a very different sense than they perceived. I say nothing here of the bewildering collections some-times found in museums that have never had the services of those experts who know something of what museums should be. Gradually we are attaining a high excellence in museum work. Still there is a tendency, even in some of the more modern institutions, to resort to quantity. I have always enjoyed a good laugh at the Florida animal farm that advertises 2,000 alligators. The alligator is an interesting reptile, and I imagine they are very fecund, so that as in the case of guinea pigs you may run up your stock pretty fast. But the menagerie

They can't see it all. Even at the visitor center information desk,
interpretation is "revelation based upon information."
(Photo by Dan Riss)

in question pretends to be no more than a menagerie; it does not style itself a museum. When people are in a holiday mood, or want to break the monotony of a long automobile trip, it is quite possible that 2,000 alligators may be just the right number, and if the quantity should drop to 1,900 there would be great disappointment.

Yet, I had the alligators vividly recalled when I attended the Hall of Fame and Baseball Museum in Cooperstown, New York, and saw a tremendous number of autographed baseballs marshalled in cases. I am personally predisposed toward baseball; it is a fine sport. It is not for me to say whether it is a pastime of sufficient importance to justify the distinction here given it. I had a fancy, during my visit, that perhaps it might better form a section of a Museum of American Sports, in which all our games would be represented. But the point I make is that the mere multiplication of autographed baseballs does not increase the interest in the exhibit. I am on dangerous ground now, for the baseball aficionado is a hot-blooded fellow who has been known to threaten the umpire with bodily injury.

What I say of baseballs seems to me equally true of churns, trivets, Currier and Ives prints, coins, stamps, indentures, or any other of thousands of items—unless, of course, the single purpose of the exhibit is to show such things as a specialty.

Another excess leads to diffusion of interest. The commonest example of this, in private life, is the agony suffered by the friends who have been invited to come over for the evening and see projected on the screen some of the pictures George and Alice have taken with their camera. They may be slides, or they may be motion strips. The lens has a most uncanny way of picking out for a beginner shooting his first color roll some of the best shots he is ever likely to achieve; but if George and Alice had edited their collection carefully the evening might have been more successful. All these pictures have equal merit in the eyes of the entertainers; the victims are rushed from a backyard cookout to the seashore, from sister's baby to the petunias, from the birdbath to the autumnal colors of a maple tree. The result is a dizziness that cannot be traced to the cocktails. You have seen nothing because you have seen everything. This is the numbness of diffusion.

I give above an absurd and extreme instance in the domestic world. But some years ago I visited a very fine historic house, lovingly

Ideally, interpretive programs and displays should be accessible to everyone.
At times, however, special accommodations must be made.
(Courtesy of National Park Service)

arranged and maintained. It had been the home of a famous author. Somewhere, during a journey abroad, the author had written a single comment: "This evening we all went to the circus." Based upon that single clue there was included among the exhibits a miniature circus. It was a very neat and charming little circus. But what possible place had it in the house? Had the author's youth been spent as a trapeze performer with Barnum, it would have been true to the biographical picture. This is diffusion.

A peculiar kind of excess in some of our scenic parks is the disposition to set up telescopes, usually operated by dropping money in a slot and serviced by a concessioner (when they are serviced at all, for frequently they are out of order and the coin is lost), with the purpose of bringing the distant objects nearer. In some cases, as when there is an extraordinary geological formation situated where it could not otherwise be seen by the visitor, such a device is clearly desirable. In general use, they minimize or defeat the opportunity to get that sweeping sense of magnificence that only the human eye, with its normal range and backed by imagination, can procure. What other reason was there for setting up this viewpoint, or developing this overlook, than that you should get the full effect, rather than to distinguish rocks and trees as individuals?

The artist draughtsmen have a neat name for pictures that labor in confusing detail. They describe them as being "too busy." I had a friend who, though a most successful illustrator for the magazines, had always had a struggle to conquer his tendency to busyness. One day when I was loafing in his studio he said to me, "You know, I was wondering last night, just before I went to sleep, if I were cast away on a desert island in the Pacific, and could bring only one tool ashore with me, what tool I should prefer that one to be."

"A knife?" I suggested, not too brightly.

"No," was the reply, "an eraser."

CHAPTER 11 🖋 The Mystery of Beauty

Doth perfect beauty stand in need of praise? Nay; no more than law,
no more than truth, no more than loving kindness, nor than modesty.
—*Marcus Aurelius,* Meditations

In the domain of aesthetics, the interpreter must be wary. It is not good to gild the lily. Not only is the lily destroyed, but the painter has made a confession that he does not understand the nature of beauty.

There is no adequate definition of beauty, though there are many noble essays; and this is true, I believe, for the reason that beauty is at once an abstraction and a reality. You might be interested in the way Bernard Bosanquet interprets the Greek philosopher Plotinus on the subject: "Beauty is all that symbolizes, in a form perceptible to the senses, laws eternally active." Immanuel Kant found that beauty (the sublime) is "that which by its . . . mightiness shocks us and fills us with pain at our own smallness, but then fills us with a feeling of the exaltation of the greatness of our own nature."

Describe it how you will, it is certain that beauty is a very real as well as an elusive thing, and it could be an element for the lack of which the human being would not care to live.

For my purpose, and as a caution to the interpreter in the whole field of aesthetics, I choose one of the best passages of Emerson: "Nature never became a toy to a wise spirit. The flowers, the animals, the mountains, reflected the wisdom of his best hour, as much as they had delighted the simplicity of his childhood."

In concrete example: if we are showing the majesty of the Teton Range, we must not do or say anything that would make a toy of this experience. These Alpine peaks know how to speak for themselves, and they speak a language that the world of people shares.

An object, whether a mountain, a lake, a crystal, a Chippendale, or a heroic act, is not made more beautiful by being called beautiful. And the perception of beauty is always in the nature of a surprise. We sometimes humorously call overlooks in the national park areas "ohs and ahs" from the fact that these exclamations are the spontaneous manner in which the visitor expresses his wonderstruck feeling. Thus, in an interpretive sign you are not wise to describe any definite object as beautiful; besides being impertinent by infringing upon the visitor's taste, you are interposing between him and the scene. But there is no harm in using a phrase like "the beauty that surrounds us in this region," for now you are establishing a mood, and the generalization, concerning which there would seldom be any disagreement, leaves the person a free choice as regards any single object.

So, I think where the interpreter is dealing with aesthetic values he will do well to restrict himself to two offices: first, to create the best possible vantage points from which beauty may be seen and comprehended; and second, to do all that discreetly may be done to establish a mood, or sympathetic atmosphere.

It may be, as Ronald Lee suggested to me, that this first endeavor is a principle of interpretation. I do not reject the idea; it may well be. But since I think of it as so greatly a matter of design, management, planning, landscaping, road construction, or whatever, I prefer to deal with it in the present manner. That it is a function of the highest importance there can be no doubt. Also, whatever may be said of the establishment of the vantage point and the mood for the contact with beauty may be said equally, though in varying degrees and by varied means, of the wilderness park, the museum, or the historic house.

Specifically, then, wherever the major aspect of the thing is aesthetic, I would have no oral or written interpretation that did more than deftly create a feeling, and rather for the whole than for a part. For the rest, it is a study for the master planner and the landscape or other architect. Mr. John D. Rockefeller Jr., with his sensitive eye for the surprise in the enjoyment of the natural scene, may err on the side of too many vistas, which, truly enough, can do some violence to the concept of unspoiled natural conditions; but I think his underlying purpose is sound and generous, both qualities characteristic of him.

We should not attempt to describe that which is only—or better—to be apprehended by feeling.

In South Carolina, the outdoor museum of sculpture called Brookgreen Gardens is the humane and artistic creation, on the site of an old plantation, of two splendid amateurs, the Huntingtons (a felicitous interpretive marker from these gardens is quoted in chapter 8). Here, as it seemed to me when I spent several happy hours there, is an instance of an institution that needs very little interpretation, oral or otherwise. There are some questions arising in the mind of the visitor, but these do not concern the aesthetic qualities and could well be answered (as perhaps they are since I was there) in a small leaflet. For the greatest part, Brookgreen Gardens is self-interpreting. The mood and the vantage ground are established in the very essence of the place.

But consider Craters of the Moon National Monument, near Arco, Idaho. Here is something that requires adept interpretation to be realized in its beauty and wonder. I say "beauty," for to me it is beautiful, since I follow John Ruskin in the thought that fitness is the first element of beauty.* But if my neighbor thinks this hurly-burly of volcanic forms is ugly, I shall not argue. We merely define beauty for ourselves differently.

Craters of the Moon pictures nature in agony. The magma could no longer be enchained; it boiled up from the depths and flowed out, and hurled itself upon the earth, cooling in astonishing forms. Since most people think of beauty as something perceivable through the eye alone, here is a challenge for the interpreter. He must take the visitor into that larger sphere of the same quality, which we may call order, or perfect compensation. His task, then, is to make a living and thrilling story of that marvelous balance maintained by nature, whereby a loss of weight in earth structure at any given spot is restored at some other, maintaining the axis we currently enjoy.

Similarly, in a steep-walled canyon on which is written the drama of ages of erosion and deposit, though the major aspect is not commonly thought to be aesthetic, the beauty of it can be made to appear in this larger sense. I sometimes wonder whether almost all of what we are trying to interpret does not fall, at last, into this realm of the aesthetic, in- and out-of-doors. Following this thought, the sod house of the Dakota settlers becomes not merely a bit of social history, but

* "Can a dung-basket," said Aristippus, "be a beautiful thing?" "Yes, by Jupiter," returned Socrates, "and a golden shield may be an ugly thing, if the one be beautifully formed for its particular uses, and the other ill formed." —Xenophon's *Memorabilia*

Describe it how you will, then, silence . . . for beauty is in the eye of the beholder.
(Photo by R. Bruce Craig)

Evening campfire programs are excellent opportunities to educate visitors and leave them with a memory that will last a lifetime. (Courtesy of National Park Service)

something beautiful, because man used to full purpose that which he found of the materials at hand. I once saw a structure in Big Bend National Park mostly built of the dry flower stalks of the agave and of ocotillo stems, roofed with rushes from the river bank. Was that not beautiful? It is when we resort to cunning inventions that we so often create the truly ugly.

I find the smithy, as seen in a number of our fine reconstructions of the village life of our past, a beautiful thing. Even the man himself, plying the bellows; the rich red that comes into what were almost dead coals; the sparks flying from under the hammer beat; the very simplicity of a muscular, fitly clothed man using expertly the rudest tools in creative work—all this is not merely history, which would be fine in itself, bringing past into present with nostalgic sweetness, but deeper than all this: the reflection of man's will to do, and his kinship with all that breathes around him, and even with the ore that sleeps in the ground, awaiting his touch.

All this the interpreter can project in simple terms, but only if he himself feels its beauty. Out of his special knowledge he can do much more, of course; but this feeling is elementary. From this, and out of his studies and his research, he molds all into a "single science" (as Socrates phrased it); and whether you wish to call this love, or beauty, or something you think less pretentious, the effect is to send the visitor away with something more than a fact, and we may call that something inspiration.

If I were arranging a museum, whether of minerals or other things, I think I should have the visitor see, as he enters, one beautiful, un-labeled thing. If it is surpassingly lovely of its own sort, it is of no consequence, at the moment, what its specific name may be. Anyone who wishes to know later will be informed. I would have ample space around it, so that nothing could jostle for supremacy. I am not a museum expert, and if it were left to me to create a whole museum, I fear I should make sad work of it. But I do feel sure that I am right about establishing the mood and the stance.

Charles Darwin was in Brazil as a scientist; but he spoke as a visitor when he wrote: "It is easy to specify the individual objects in these grand scenes; but it is not possible to give an adequate idea of the higher feelings of wonder, astonishment and devotion, which fill and elevate the mind."

If a man of science could so feel, then the finest uses of national parks, or indeed of any of the preserves that come within the range of interpretive work, lie ultimately in spiritual uplift. This end cannot be reached except through a walk with beauty of some aspect, in which the interpreter is not primarily a teacher, but a companion in the adventure.

CHAPTER 12

🍃 The Priceless Ingredient

Like a great poet, Nature produces the greatest effects with the fewest
materials—sun, trees, flowers, water and love; that is all. If, indeed the
last is wanting in the heart of the beholder, the whole is likely to seem to
him a daub; the sun is only so many miles in diameter, the trees are good
for firewood, the flowers are classified by the number of their stamens,
and the water is—wet. —Heinrich Heine, Die Harzreise

Henry James, in his very un-Jameslike book *A Little Tour in France*, gives a humorous description of the "interpretation" provided at the ancient Cité of Carcassonne, in Provence: "It was not to be denied that there was a relief in separating from our accomplished guide, whose manner of imparting information reminded me of the energetic process by which I have seen mineral waters bottled." After escaping from the guide, James "treated himself" to another walk around the citadel—alone.

We all know this guide as though he had fizzed in our presence. We have met his like—a little better, perhaps, but also perhaps a little worse. Such guides are not all in France. I am reminded of a party of visitors I joined to explore a limestone cave. The guide was amiable and personable, but he had made two major mistakes in the work he was pursuing—without catching. In the first place, he had committed a recital to memory, and he suffered a lapse of memory before he had got very far. This may be a source of embarrassment to the interpreter, but it is worse for his auditors, for they not merely bleed with him—they bleed for him. After that agonizing stoppage, our guide said, "Well, I'll begin again . . ." This time he sailed through.

But the second defect was the fatal one. He had undertaken this interpretive work without being in love. If you love the thing you interpret, and love the people who come to enjoy it, you need commit nothing to memory. For, if you love the thing, you not only have taken the pains to understand it to the limit of your capacity, but you also feel its special beauty in the general richness of life's beauty. This, to be sure, may make you tend to overemphasize your particular task;

but the fault is corrected as you come to know more about the limits of time, absorptive abilities, and a just proportion.

Before going farther, I must explain definitely what I mean by a "love of people." Precisely I do not imply any mushy view of humankind, or an exaggerated notion of their virtues. In the course of a long career, the interpreter will meet the pestiferous, the unmanageable, the ineducable, and some whose apparent reason for existence is to provide the hangman with work. These are not the many; they are the few. One who has suffered a number of attacks by poison ivy may get the idea that this malicious plant dominates the scenery. In truth it occupies only a little space in the whole floral luxuriance.

The interpreter will not abase himself, he will insist upon being treated with respect, and he will have no taint of mock humility. He will be humble, not because he is overawed by his contacts, but only because he falls short, in his own judgment, of the flying perfect at which he aims.

No, indeed; you are not to love people in any sickly sense. You are to love people in the sense that you never cease trying to understand them and to realize that whatever faults they have, whatever levity, whatever ignorance, they are not peculiar. People were not born with the special purpose of making an interpreter uncomfortable. "There, but for the grace of God, go I," said the prelate as he saw the criminal marched to his doom.

Samuel Taylor Coleridge has explained this to me, who have needed the explanation as much as, and perhaps more than, any: "If you do not understand a man's ignorance," said Coleridge, "you will remain ignorant of his understanding."

When first I read those words, I confess it sounded to me like a verbal trick. But later the essential truth, the vital importance of it for interpretation, dawned upon me. The interpreter will have no difficulty in translating this aphorism in terms of his own experience. The visitors who come for his services have seldom any expert, or even moderate, knowledge of the things they come to see or to experience. They come frequently with mere idle curiosity, or to kill time, or from boredom. It is for us to understand, and affectionately to weigh, not the ignorance, for that is apparent, but the reasons for the ignorance.

Compared with the usual fate of humans, we who are engaged in preservation work, daily in contact with what we most like and admire, are fortunate indeed. As I write this, I have just returned from a gathering of men and women in the museum and historic-house field. What cheerful, rapt faces! What intensity of interest! What freedom of discussion, where difference of opinion about procedure was taken for granted and met with a smile. Do you really think this is common experience in the workaday world? Are you unaware of the fact that most people often feel that they are traveling the wrong road, and bitterly conclude that it is too late to return to a distant fork?

You cannot change this, but you can understand it; and thus you can account for the poor conditioning of those whom you would delight with an introduction to the treasures in your custody. There is the challenge! To put your visitor in possession of at least one disturbing idea that may grow into a fruitful interest.

Carl Feiss, the city planner, told me that when he was visiting a historic house he observed that a number of people asked the identical question: "Is this place still in the hands of the same family?" There, at least, is a vulnerable spot that most people share in common: the longing for continuity, whether it be of ownership of real estate, of their own family or race, or of the subtler kind that relates the puzzled human to the physical world he sees about him.

Thus, when the interpreter comes to understand the basis of the *ignorance* of his visitor, he is prepared to deal with that auditor's *understanding*. And the understanding is usually ample; only its range is entirely outside, at first glance, what the interpreter knows and feels concerning his wares. When I was guiding hundreds of people through the Castillo in St. Augustine, it was not difficult to look into the eyes of those who sat before me in the orientation room off the sally port and register the effect I was producing. There was a man who seemed impenetrable until I came to mention the manner in which the great blocks of coquina (shell) rock, quarried on Anastasia Island just across the bay, were used in the construction. Suddenly this man shot a question at me: "How were they *bonded*?" Fortunately, I knew the meaning of the term as he used it, and I was able to explain that the cementing material was at hand for the builders in the form of sharp sand and oyster shells. From that moment he was interested in the fort. He came to me afterward and said, "I want to know more about this. Can you suggest a book about it?" He was

*After their visit, visitors often seek additional information
on their own. Visitor center bookstores and gift shops are an
essential extension of the interpretive experience.
(Photo by R. Bruce Craig)*

a building constructor, and I had touched him where he lived. I had reached his understanding. Now he was on the high road to history.

Enough of this aspect of love; and now to the love of his subject that the interpreter must possess. "To know a thing," wrote Thomas Carlyle, "what we can call *knowing*, a man must first *love* the thing, sympathize with it: that is, be virtuously related to it." Priceless ingredient, indeed.

I think of a letter written by Frank Pinkley, the first superintendent of the Southwestern National Monuments Office in the National Park Service. It was not my good fortune to know "Boss" Pinkley, as he was known affectionately, but none other than an extraordinary lover of his work could have left such an impress upon his associates that they cannot mention him without a moistening of eye and a little quaver of voice. Here is Pinkley writing of one of his subordinates who had just left the world:

> I was startled the other day to get the news that Park Supervisor Gabriel Sovulewski was no longer on the active list. . . . His park never became commonplace to him . . . he once took me on a geological trip on the floor of the Valley, which wound up at the foot of Capitan. We sat there three or four minutes; wordless; drinking it all in; and then he said something I have never forgotten: "You can talk all you want to about how this valley was formed, but there is where your science ends and Almighty God begins."

This reverence for what, in our natural world of fitness and beauty, is not factual but of the spirit; for that which is beyond diction; for the very soul of that which the interpreter makes a living and potent reality in a cloudy experience—this reverence is brought into interpretation by love.

"White Mountains" Smith, an old-timer among national park rangers, expressed his love in an explosive way. Tom Vint tells me that one day he was riding the upper road in Jackson Hole with Smith, when the latter suddenly wheeled his car off into the brushy shoulder, jumped out and drew Tom after him. He swept his arm along the horizon line of the incomparable Tetons and blurted: "By God, Tom, I call that beautiful!" Understand, Smith had seen that jagged horizon line day after day. Far from being jaded, his love saw new beauties every time he looked. Even if his expression was characteristically rugged, you do not need my suggestion that it was as truly reverent as that of Gabriel Sovulewski, companion of "Boss" Pinkley.

Whether the interpreter is placed in primitive surrounding, or at a battlefield, or among the ruins of Pueblo people, or in a house that has sheltered a continuing family for two centuries and a half—all is one. If he is "virtuously related" to it, as Carlyle said, he can people the historic house, the ruins, the battlefield; and in our primeval parks, by the magic of love, he can create the feeling in his hearers that this is the virgin wilderness, with all its associated plant and animal life, which was first glimpsed by the hardy trappers and explorers pushing westward in dangerous but joyous adventure.

In a field where so much specific thinking and action is constantly required, I do not wish to take my readers into a rarefied atmosphere if it can be avoided. But Socrates had a sweep of vision that I am continually finding referable to true interpretation, and I am going to risk a quotation. Socrates said that the prophetess Diotima told him what follows; but Socrates often had tongue in cheek. I think he and Diotima were the same person.

> Love is something more than the desire of beauty; it is the instinct of immortality in a mortal creature. . . . He who has the instinct of true love, and can discern the relations of true beauty in every form, will go on from strength to strength until at last the vision is revealed to him of *a single science*, and he will suddenly perceive a nature of wondrous beauty in the likeness of no human face or form, but absolute, simple, separate and everlasting.

Now, I should be somewhat less than honest if I were to pretend that I understand in fullness what Socrates meant by the above. I rather think that Benjamin Jowett, who so admirably translated the Platonic works, was himself occasionally puzzled. Maybe the Greeks had an intellectual slant that does not quite exist in the modern world. But I have the satisfying feeling that a tremendous truth is here involved.

The word "physis" underwent a number of changes in Greek thought until it came to mean pretty much what we call "nature." I am sure that over the centuries to come, the word "interpretation" will similarly change its meanings to cover a broadened horizon of thinking and to fit new needs and practices.

For the moment, I see in the quoted words of Diotima a curious likeness to the present stage, at least, of our interpretation, when it is good. We start from related or unrelated fact and strive toward a revealing generalization, but finally simplify again in the direction of a statement, or projection of a feeling, that will satisfy any situation because it deals with some element of interest common to all our preservations and common to all visitor experience.

Thus, the six principles with which I began this book may be after all (like the "single science" mentioned by Socrates) a single principle. If this should be so, I feel certain that the single principle must be love.

CHAPTER 13

🍃 Of Gadgetry

Archimedes: Give me a fulcrum and I will move the world.
Diogenes: Will it be better off in some other place?

When I use the word "gadget" I mean no disrespect. I am writing this on a gadget; I hope I am not ungrateful, for it saves me the trouble of pushing, with cramped fingers, a quill pen. I am sometimes persuaded that the best writing that ever will be done was in the time of the stylus or the pen-and-foolscap; but if that be true, it could owe, conceivably, to a decadence in the writers. Anyhow, since this book is more concerned with the thinking about interpretation than the excellence of expression, the point has no large importance.

The fact with which I deal is that, in the field of interpretation, the gadget has come to stay and will be used to a much greater extent than is now the case. There will never be a device of telecommunication as satisfactory as the direct contact not merely with the voice, but with the hand, the eye, the casual and meaningful ad lib, and with that something which flows out of the very constitution of the individual in his physical self. While I think nobody disagrees upon this, we all know that there will not be enough of those individuals to make the direct contact. We shall catch up with a current requirement only to find ourselves behind again. So, whether one likes it or not, we are going to have more—and I should hope, better—mechanical devices aimed at multiplying the interpretive effort.

This means, explicitly, more automatic projection equipment, more sound installations, more recorders and tapes, more gadgets to be self-operated by visitors, more motion pictures of fidelity and professional skill, and so on.

I was in some doubt as to whether a chapter on this subject properly belonged in the kind of book I am writing, because it is apparent that such a mechanical device can never deliver anything better than what some person thought, prepared, spoke, or otherwise personally performed. Indeed, it must be, in spite of any electronic perfection of the machine, always a shade toward the worse. The gadget is a willing slave, and repeats even your intake of breath, your *hem*'s and *ha*'s, and your stumbles from the ideal in every way. If I spell "cat" with a *k* on my typewriter, it is not the machine's defect.

Yet, in my long course of study of interpretation, which has taken me so many thousands of miles and into so many and varied preserved areas, I have arrived at some reflections concerning the present use of mechanical devices, and it may be of some little service to announce them here.

1. No device of the kind we here consider is, other things being equal, as desirable as interpretation by direct contact with the person. (I shall not further discuss this, for practically everybody agrees; but it is a good point to start from.)
2. A good device is far better than no contact at all.
3. A good result by device is better than a poor performance by an individual.
4. A poor interpretation by mechanical means is worse than a poor interpretation by personal contact.
5. A poor interpretation by mechanical means is not necessarily better than none at all; it may be worse than none at all, for you may add the same insult to injury as when one imposes upon another person a time-wasting telephone call.
6. No institution should install any mechanical devices until it knows that such gadgets can be adequately, continually, and quickly serviced. No matter how good they may be when they are working properly, they are a source of shame and chagrin, as well as an imposition on the public, when they are allowed to be more than briefly inoperative.

Not long ago I went into a city-owned museum where, in the section devoted to geology, there was a well-selected group of fluorescent minerals in a black-light cabinet. Personally, I delight—even with a child's delight—in these lovely specimens. But the device was not working. I sought one of the employees, who told me in a courteous but rather weary tone that "it went out of order very easily." His manner clearly suggested to me that it had not been working for some time, and it might be another long time before anything was done about it. So as far as fluorescence was concerned, this device might as well have been stored in the cellar.

The visitor center helps set the stage for the visitor experience. Here, one can often view an orientation film and gain an overview of the experience to come. (Photo by R. Bruce Craig)

*In a museum setting, the interpreter seldom comes into direct contact
with the visitor. Consequently, the medium and the message are one.
(Photo by R. Bruce Craig)*

I attended a campfire talk in one of our national parks when the visitors, on the first occasion I was present, waited more than half an hour because the voice amplifier was out of order. The folks who attend these campfire talks, I have found, are very patient and grateful for the interpretation offered them; so they were on this occasion. I went to the same place on the following two nights, because each program offered was interesting to me. There was the same mechanical trouble; the same delay. It occurred to me then that actually the amplifier was not needed at all. The circle was small. The amplifier, when it did operate, was badly adjusted and unpleasant. Any one of the speakers I heard (and two of them were uncommonly good, with well-selected slides) could have made himself heard perfectly without resort to a mechanism. We cannot too much stress the fact that any amplification is at best a necessary evil, and that the average speaker with a minimum of proper training can make himself perfectly intelligible without unusual effort where the space is not too great. I shall go no farther into this feature, since there is plenty of literature on the subject.

Finally, in the resort to mechanical devices there is another danger to be avoided. An interpreter confided to me that he looked with pleasure on the coming of such automation because "it will give me more time for research." It should be obvious that this is not the proper purpose. My comment is not to be understood as meaning that the interpreter should not indulge in research if he has the talent for it. He may, on the contrary, very profitably do so. I mean simply that the reason stated is not a good one. In this instance a practical consideration was involved. The current need of the area was for firsthand oral interpretation, not research.

Gadgets do not supplant the personal contact; we accept them as valuable alternatives and supplements.

CHAPTER 14

🌿 The Happy Amateur

> *In the word amateur there is something lovable, which gives a congenial*
> *aspect to the person of whom it is said. With pleasure we say of someone:*
> *"he is an amateur," whereby we envision immediately a happy man,*
> *a smiling Maecenas, living among beautiful things and appreciating*
> *them.*
>
> *And what, in truth, is an amateur? First, and above all, he is one*
> *who finds a consuming interest in studies that are quite aside from his*
> *regular work.* — *Pierre Humbert*

Over the years words undergo wear and tear, and some of them emerge the worse for it. When Samuel Johnson wrote his dictionary, the word "officious" meant "kindly; helpful." Now if you call a man officious, he is insulted, for you imply that he is an impertinent meddler. When French explorer Samuel de Champlain wrote that Mount Desert Island—now containing Acadia National Park—was "inhabité," he meant that it was a wilderness, exactly the opposite of what we now mean by the word.

But, to me, the saddest fate of any has been suffered by the word "amateur." I am not sure just at what period the fine old noun was perverted for common usage. To most people now it means a dabbler, a bungler, a producer of something inferior. What a pity! For this word once described a person who could not be otherwise than happy, since he was doing something for the love of it; not for material gain, not even for fame or pre-eminence: he or she simply gave the head and heart, and rejoiced. A hobby? No, more than a hobby; though a good hobby has often added years to a life. No; something of higher meaning, more satisfying to the soul. We shall see.

First, let us consider the dire need for the revival of the amateur spirit. In the past several years there has come into our general magazines a flood of articles dealing with the acute problem of American social life arising from the vast increase of leisure time. This problem engages the thought of the sociologist, the economist, and even the psychiatrist. "Are you a week-end neurotic?" is the title of a recent inquiry. The point seemed to be that millions of Americans, having looked forward keenly to the release from their work, find themselves in the clutch of "a deep-seated fear of relaxation and leisure . . . creating feelings of uneasiness, and sometimes of acute illness." The reason is obvious enough: the victims of this weekend moodiness have had no training in the fruitful and pleasurable use of leisure. But knowing the explanation does not supply the corrective. Unplanned, uninspired free time can be a curse, and we need only to refer to the experience of the Romans to find a practical realization of the fact. The successful Mithridatic wars brought into a conventional hard-working Roman polity a tide of slaves and treasure from the East. There was indeed plenty of leisure as a result. But it ended in donatives (doles) and a social instability that even the ablest autocrats of the Empire were unable to stifle.

Today we are dealing neither with imported slaves nor with the fatness of conquest, but through productive shortcuts we reach the same end of more and more leisure.

By contrast, the Greeks of the "golden" period (that of Pericles, let us say) seem to have had a considerable knowledge of the profitable use of their leisure. There were slaves in Athens, too, and a large body besides of people who were neither slave nor franchised. The Greeks of the period certainly had enough faults, but by all accounts they possessed a happy versatility that permitted them to be amateurs of music, of the theatre, of oratory, and of the finesse of logical discussion, and even (if you trust Aristophanes) to have a passion for sitting on juries and enjoy legal hairsplitting. At any rate, you get no idea that the Athenian was bored on his "weekend." In a republic that produced such consummate artists and thinkers, it must have been that the people liked it that way. They were a crowd of happy amateurs. Those that could not create, could appreciate and encourage. Happy versatility!

Now, if these observations are substantially correct, they have a vital importance for all those earnest administrators of, and workers in, the national, state, and other parks, the publicly and privately owned museums, historic houses—all preserves where some measure of interpretation is involved and practiced. For, the thoughtful administrator of such preserves, as well as the interpreter intent upon doing his utmost to realize their greatest possibilities to mind and spirit, is constantly checking and rechecking himself with the blunt and honest question: "Just what is it that I am trying to do? What is the place of this institution, of which I am a part, in the scheme of American life?"

Protection and preservation of the physical memorials of our natural and historic origins is primary, of course. And I suppose a good case could be made for the mere locking-up of our most important treasures—the fragile and the irreplaceable and the "bank deposits" of study in future years—because they are the arks of our covenants and even when not seen are an inspiration through the feeling that they exist and are safe.

But, unfortunately, save in rare instances, this is not at all required. We can *use* these precious resources, so long as we do not *use them up*. Put it this way: we should not dissipate our capital, but we should zealously dispense the interest.

Ah, but how? That is what the interpreter wants to know. A good generalization would be: we maintain these preserves so that all the people will have access to the source material of our natural and historic origins, besides having the relaxation and novelty of coming into a world apart from their daily round, and into the presence of beauty, art, the significant moment, and the stirring event. But how is this laudable purpose to be translated into a continuing interest that does not end, but really begins, when our visitor has left the park, the museum, or the historic place?

Even if it were desirable—and it is not—to create a nation of accomplished specialists through visits to such places, the interpreter knows that this is impossible. The take-home acquisition of direct education derived by the visitor is pitifully small, for he has not come to be educated. He has come to see, to sample, to try something new. Is Grand Canyon really as wonderful as Joe Smith told me? He has heard that "everybody ought to visit" Fort Laramie, or the Vanderbilt Mansion, or Monticello. "All right; I am here. Show me."

The visitor doesn't know it, but he has walked into a delightful trap. From his very curiosity and vagueness of purpose, he has given the interpreter a chance. What chance? Well, certainly not to send him away with a packet of specific information. If he should happen to be at Fort Laramie National Historic Site, he will not remember whether a certain unfortunate commander's name was Fetterman, or Winckelman, or Peabody, or what year the fort was established. No; the opportunity is to make a happy amateur of him by thrilling him with the story of the great western trek of the American; the plodding of the hobnailed boots over the Oregon Trail toward the sunset; the conquest of the West; the flowering of the Territories. The tale of Laramie is a significant part, but the whole picture is the one that may engage your visitor in a love that will take care of his leisure time.

We do have such happy amateurs already; many and many of them; but far, far from enough for our national welfare. Have you heard of the groups called "The Westerners"? There are your happy amateurs! There may be qualified historians among them, but most are men of many trades who get together, not merely to toss a glass and eat a snack, but to match minds in the fascinating historical quest of which they are all lovers. So it is with the many who gather at what are called the "Civil War Round Tables." If you have ever attended one of these meetings, you could never suppose any one of the amateurs of our domestic war would be at a loss to employ his leisure time with delight. There may be, for all I know, neurotics among them, but the neurosis does not arise for such a reason.

And somehow this reminds me that one does not need the background of a formal education to become an amateur of either art or science. The case of Marc Navarrete and his father, Fred, who live on a ranch near Naco, Arizona, is a cheerful instance of this fact. Of these two men, Dr. Emil W. Haury, of the University of Arizona, has written: "The exemplary attitude and the alertness of the Navarretes shine as a beacon on the relationship between the interested amateur and the specialist. It is my sincere hope that the vital part these men have played in adding to a clearer understanding of Early Man in the Southwest will be a lasting satisfaction to them."

Fred and Marc Navarrete had for some fifteen years been watching an arroyo eroded by Greenbush Creek, as it widened and deepened. I do not know how the Navarretes became interested in archaeology. But it certainly could have been due to a visit to one of the National Park Service archaeological areas in the Southwest. At all events, Marc Navarrete brought word to the Arizona State Museum in September 1951 of his discovery of two large projectile points in close association with mammoth bones. Being a true amateur, he knew the importance of what he had found. Likewise, being a true amateur, he realized that further exploration was for the specialists. The subsequent digging on Greenbush Creek and the finding of eight projectile points clearly indicating a prehistoric "kill" and butchering at least 10,000 years ago was, as Emil Haury says, "a triumph of the amateur spirit." Can you suppose the Navarettes become restless and ill because they find their weekends a bore?

I have indicated, early in this chapter, a difference between the hobbyist and the amateur. I have no sneers against hobbies. The hobbyist may, and frequently does, develop into a fine amateur. But I think, generally speaking, the man with a hobby is interested in *things*, while the amateur is engaged primarily with *ideas* or *culture*. The collection of coins, for example, is a hobby, and a worthy one. But when you have assembled large American pennies of every date and mint, that job is complete. If you are not tired of it, you start again with another kind of coin.

But suppose you dabble in antique coins, Greek or Roman. Long before your accumulation embarrasses your finances, you find yourself, through these coins, becoming acquainted with the social and economic life of these nations of the past. I am not a numismatist; but when I see on a Roman coin the word *Annona* or the word *Liberalitas* I know that I am being told a story of the gradual bankruptcy of the Empire, and I can see in an adulterated "silver" coin of Gallienus the end of that economic dance when the emperors had no more dole money to quiet the mobs.

With Greek coins it is the same. You begin to understand why the "owl" of Athens was eagerly sought by the other states that had tinkered with their currency. It was "good" money; even in the silliest political moments of the Athenians, they avoided debasing the bird of Minerva. Pereskius, one of the learned men of the late Renaissance, used ancient coins to study ancient history; and Pereskius was not a professional but an amateur historian.

The opportunities arising to create happy amateurs seem to me to be almost innumerable in the natural and scientific areas of the national and state and municipal parks. Already we have many hundreds of thousands of people who delight in birds, in rocks and min-

Visitors learn about their natural environment through the eyes of a naturalist, who is a jack-of-all-trades and often a master of several. (Courtesy of National Park Service)

erals, in flowers and trees, even in meteorology, with no intention whatever of making a profession of such interests.

Recently there was a news dispatch, widely printed, originating in Ottawa, Canada:

WHOOPING CRANES HAVE NOT ARRIVED

You might think, in the midst of whirling world politics, that nobody would care a whoop whether the whooping cranes had arrived anywhere, or even that they had left anywhere. But news agencies do not squander lineage. And, indeed, that bit of news came close to many people who, to be sure, will never see a whooping crane, but who are amateurs of wildlife in the noblest possible way. Because wildlife is part of our precious record of evolution, and because, as Professor J. Arthur Thompson said, "these humbler creatures are wrapped up in the bundle of life with ourselves," not a single species should be permitted to perish—at least not because of any fault of ours.

The growth of interest in rocks and minerals, especially on the part of children, has in the past quarter century been simply astounding. It continues at a rapid rate, and not long ago the manufacturer of a breakfast cereal tried the experiment of enclosing a mineral specimen in each package, with the promise of supplying a number of others. The samples were insignificant in size and needed some reference to make them important; yet it was a strangely humane and intelligent device to spring from modern advertising.

Here, again, I suggest the difference between the mere desire to make a collection of something (a good thing in its way) and the amateur spirit that deals with larger and more satisfying concepts. It is quite possible to assemble a cabinet of very fine crystals—of quartz, tourmalines, garnets, and the like—and never give much thought to the mystery of our inorganic partners of life. It is when you hold even an unshowy bit of rock in hand and consider that this sort of thing made our own life possible by being broken down into soil by tiny plants, by sun and snow and other agencies; when you sit upon a stayed boulder left by glaciation, and consider the time when plants and wildlife, and perhaps even man in our own country, had to move southward away from an increasing frigidity he could not understand; when rocks and minerals begin to add up to a big sum in our own frail origins—then you are on the way toward the status of a happy amateur. If you have ever seen a busload of "rock-hounds" clambering over some old quarry or mine dump, or attended one of their meetings when they swapped specimens and experiences, you would conclude that at least some part of our population does not become neurotic because it cannot measure up to its holiday spell.

Let us look the facts in the eye: there is at the moment more leisure time than the majority of people seem to be able to convert to the enrichment of mind and spirit. There will be more leisure time, apparently, in days to come. The formal institutions of education direct little or no effort to fill this void. I am not saying that they should. Perhaps it is indeed their business to produce effective specialists, intelligent producers of goods or means. I am sure you would annoy the ordinary educator if you suggested that he install a course in the highest uses of leisure time.

As for what is called "adult education," this seems to tend, whatever its worth, in the same direction. It fills crevices that were left through misfortune, lack of opportunity, lethargy, or slow development; but the end seems to be about the same: to make a better worker or specialist. And you still have the weekend with you.

It seems to me that in this circumstance the great hope for aiding people in the direction of a happy and fruitful use of leisure is to be found in the national parks, the state and local parks, the museums and other cultural preserves. And, by the same token, I think that here lies the greatest challenge to the interpreter who works in this field: what to do; what to say; how to point the way; how to connect the visitor's own life with something, even one thing, among all the custodial treasures; how finally to elicit from the aimless visitor the specific thought: "This is something I believe I could get interested in." Well, there lies an ideal to work for. But of one thing I am sure: it cannot be done merely by displaying wares, not by imparting mere facts. The thing is a thing of the spirit; and, to indulge in a rash paraphrase, it must be directed in spirit and in truth.

As to the "happy amateur," I am aware that I have exaggerated a little. We cannot at best do quite that for everybody. I say the ideal is good, though. And let us try to redeem that fine word "amateur" from its stained condition: shine it up and use it wealthily.

Remember, Benjamin Franklin was an amateur. He stood before

For Tilden, encouraging every visitor to a park or historic site to become a "happy amateur" is an interpretive "ideal to work for." (National Park Service photo by M. Woodbridge Williams)

kings, he was a member of scientific societies, he was inventor, he was diplomat, he was man of politics and letters; but when he wrote his will, he began, "I, Benjamin Franklin, printer . . ."

Printing was Franklin's craft; in the other fields, he regarded himself as a happy amateur. The other accomplishments richly engaged his leisure time.

CHAPTER 15 🌿 Vistas of Beauty

Truth, and goodness, and beauty, are but different faces of the same All.
Beauty in nature is not ultimate. It is the herald of inward and eternal
beauty . . . it must stand as a part and not yet as the last or highest
expression of the final cause of Nature. —Ralph Waldo Emerson

In February 1965 President Lyndon Baines Johnson sent to the Congress of the United States a message "On the Natural Beauty of Our Country." It was a state paper probably unique in the history of government. Can anyone recall a similar instance when a nation's leader has proclaimed the vital importance of beauty in human welfare and moved to salvage what remains of the lovely heritage that a thrusting, feverish, ruthless technology has dilapidated to the point of ugliness? This is a Great Chart. And the time to preserve, to repair, to cease being a nation of prosperous slovens, is now.

The German poet Goethe said, "We should do our utmost to encourage the Beautiful, for the Useful encourages itself." Indeed, utility needs nothing other than its physical materials to work upon. We need not quarrel with that. And it was inevitable that the primeval landscape of America would be vastly altered; that the rich resources would be eagerly tapped and exploited; that rivers should be harnessed, prairies plowed, that roads should scar the land surface, that virgin forests should fall. Nor could it be expected that, except for a few souls gifted with insight, a people aiming at a fuller and more comfortable existence would exercise a philosophic restraint. There is no deep villain in this very human drama. There is only a saddening imbalance that was bound to ensue. Man does not live by bread and gadgets alone. Take beauty out of his life: a googol of dollars and a Lucullan luxury will not fill the void.

The imbalance is here. It is shockingly manifest. Because of an erupting population, we see the places of natural beauty retreating from the millions as fast as they seek and move toward them; urban slums where people feebly degenerate; roadways lined with the horrible corpses of junked automobiles and with the vulgarities of clamoring commerce; our air polluted with fumes and our rivers and lakes and estuaries so laden with filth and chemicals that fish are killed and humans endangered. The whole drab picture is outlined in President Johnson's message, in measured terms.

Will the president's appeal be effective? There are already signs that it will. The regeneration will take time. Nature repairs ills of the abused human body by slow processes; ills of the spirit even more slowly. There are signs of awakening on all political levels. But it is a warning that must come into the realization of every citizen. Josiah Royce said that the philosopher Immanuel Kant "had small interest in noble sentiments, but very great natural respect for large and connected personal and social undertakings, when guided by ideas." The point is timely. The appeal for the restoration of beauty to her rightful eminence cannot remain merely a "noble sentiment." It needs action, and not merely in the field of legislation; it must enter the understanding of all of us.

II

But the message to the Congress has far wider significance than appears upon its surface, or in its words. What *is* natural beauty? What, indeed, is *beauty*?

The wisest philosophers have failed to define or to explain this human emotion to which, in our English language, is given the name of beauty. There is an equivalent word in every language. Paul Shorey, reflecting his study of Plato, said that feeling for beauty is "a touch of noble unrest; the reaching for something of finer quality than the dailiness of life." The love of beauty, he added, becomes the guide toward the perception of the Good and the True. Vague as this may seem, at first glance, it will serve as the path along which our quest for understanding must go. Surely we deal with an essence that is beyond our powers of expression. But we can, and we do, feel its reality.

In the realm of natural beauty, apprehended through the sense of sight mainly, but also by the other organs, we are first overwhelmed by the more spectacular forms. "Breathtaking" is a hackneyed expression; yet it is accurate. The pulse reflects the surge. Beyond that impact, we can come to understand that what we have sensed is only a gorgeous greeting. Behind that curtain lies an infinite world of detailed beauties. As we develop realization of those composing elements, we know that there can be nothing ugly in nature. Nothing. The seeming exceptions are simply facets of beauty we have not yet grasped.

Sometimes we think in our egotism that nature has provided these beauties as a special act on our behalf. If I may be allowed a harmless bit of fantasy, I shall imagine a conversation you might have with nature on this point. After hearing you patiently on the subject of beauty, nature would perhaps say something like this:

"I see the source of your error. It derives from your very limited knowledge. You are thinking that I have a Department of Beauty—that I deal with beauty as one of my activities. Really, I do not *intend* beauty. I *am* beauty. I am beauty and many other things, such as you are trying to express by your abstractions like Order, Harmony, Truth, Love. What you see in my scenic manifestations is the glamour behind which lies an Absolute Beauty of which I myself am an expressive part. You do not understand? Naturally it is difficult. But you are trying: I do like *that* in you, little man."

No, we can only shadowly comprehend, and perhaps the mystery will always tantalize us. But, fortunately for our spiritual welfare, we live with the Fact. And this Fact is, that in the presence of unsullied, unexploited, "raw" nature, we are lifted to a height beyond ourselves. Our first physical contact with Yosemite, with the Tetons, the redwood groves, the Alps, the falls of the Iguazu—with such spectacles wherever they exist—leaves us with an indelible coloring such as has not dominated our thoughts and feelings before. That is the Fact. The metaphysical reasoning about it is more engaging than important. We grow in dimension and capacity. Not only that. We become more sensitive to the opposite of beauty: ugliness, defacement, disharmony.

Although the purely aesthetic aspect of this Absolute Beauty is but the prologue to a whole, its importance must not be minimized. It is as basic as the letters of the alphabet. Without those letters there are no words; and without words no communication.

III

While our people have been remiss in the sacrifice of beauty to utility, and the time has come to take account of stock, as the president asked, there is still much to our credit. In a period of explosive growth such as few nations have known, possessors of a technological skill that has finally become more than a little frightening, we have yet managed to set aside and wisely to administer a system of national parks that evokes the admiration of the world. It is true that we had rare advantages, and time was on our side. But it is also true that we had from our earliest days a large and articulate group of forward-thinking men and women alive to the need for preserving the treasures of our culture and the integrity of our inheritance before, as in other lands, it was too late. So that, as the case stands, it is not so much that we have been unmindful of spiritual and moral values: we have not been sufficiently alert to the somber truth that "the Useful encourages itself," while the preservation and affirmation of beauty needs a constant renewal of faith and the watchful devotion of a shepherd. Nor can our preserved places of natural beauty and memorials of the historic past prosper and remain inspirational if they become islands in an environment of sanctioned ugliness. This is a very nullification of our reverence for beauty. To paraphrase Lincoln: our cultural and spiritual aspirations must shrivel in a world half beautiful, half loathsome. We shall not expect the impossible. But there must be in our mechanized and controlled ecology, while we confess that we have violated much natural beauty physically, and defend it as unavoidable, a manifestation that we still retain the spirit, and show it in our national housekeeping. That is where we have failed.

IV

As I have said, this message is something not merely for legislation, though that is imperatively desirable, but for all of us to meditate. What are its implications, for example, in the work of the National Park System, where so much natural beauty, majestic and awe inspiring, and so many less obvious beauties, even hidden ones, are the current stock-in-trade? The very business of the Natural Park Service is the custodianship and interpretation of beauty. How could it be otherwise? The interpreter, whether naturalist or ranger or historian or mechanic, is a middleman of this precious cultural wealth.

Viewed as an absolute, beauty has numberless aspects. For the purpose of the interpreter, I think we need be directly concerned with but four.

1. *The park visitor's sensuous contact with scenic or landscape beauty—with "wildness."* It is axiomatic that natural beauty, as perceived by the organs of sense, needs no interpretation: it interprets itself. Here the interpreter acts only as a scout and a guide. He leads his groups to the most alluring scenes he has discovered, and is silent. Would you varnish the orchid? He refrains even from using the word "beauty." To suggest that his visitors are to consider either the scene or the song of the hermit thrush as beautiful is even an affront. They *know*. In this aspect beauty is a precious personal possession. It is the individual's shock, *his* apprehension, *his* discovery: and what he discovers is more than what he sees or hears. He has discovered something of himself, hitherto unrealized. No; we do not interpret that aspect of beauty. It is an exhibit.

2. *The beauty of the adventure of the mind: the revelation of the order of nature.* Exactly at this point is where the office of the interpreter begins. There is a concealed beauty that does not appear to the senses. Indeed, this aspect takes two forms. It involves a revelation of the natural beauty we think of as order—nature at work—and the beauty of that development of the human mind that makes it possible for man partly to understand it. What are the forces that created what one sees, and feels, as beautiful?

In this book my aim has been, besides giving a working definition of interpretation, to lay down a set of principles that should be in the mind of the interpreter. As to my definition, I have never been wholly happy, but nobody has seemed to offer a better one, so I rest with it. But, as to the face-to-face communication that the field interpreter is privileged to have with the millions who come to our parks, I have come to feel that I missed something—a factor of extreme importance.

Whether we call it so or not, the interpreter is engaged in a kind of education. It is not the classroom kind. It is, if you will, a proffer of teaching; but it is not the professorial sort. It aims not to *do something* to the listener, but *to provoke the listener to do something to him-*

self. It is a delicate job, requiring the greater discretion. The man on holiday does not wish to be lectured; he did not come to a park to be educated. Even the most discerning, and therefore, successful, interpreter must feel conscious of the fact that the materials upon which he works are by their very nature—what shall I say? Not *cold*, but certainly *cool*. We appeal to the head, to the mind.

Can we not infuse into this worthy activity an appeal to the heart: to attain something of that impact that nature does so easily and implicitly by presenting the beautiful landscape? Erosion and mountain building, the adaptation of life to its environment, the grand and vital organic community of which man is only a species, however a dominant one—all these entertaining revelations of man's place in nature are at last a presentation of an aspect of the beautiful. If the interpreter feels this to be so, he can project that feeling. Not by a preachment about it. Heavens, no. It is something to be felt, not analyzed. If deeply felt, it can be communicated.

The scenes upon which you have looked, and the natural sounds you have heard, you regard as beauty. How did it all come about? By a process that science aims to know more and more about; but whatever we may discover, one thing is sure about that process—it is even more beautiful than that that the eye or ear perceives. This is an appeal to the heart, the soul, or whatever you wish to call it, which constantly yearns to be satisfied. It is warmth. Added to understanding, it is the objective of interpretation.

A great American chemist, Robert S. Mulliken, who received a Nobel Prize in 1966, once wrote something that has deeply affected my thinking about the world of natural beauties: "The scientist must develop enormous tolerance in seeking for ideas which *may please nature*, and enormous patience, self-restraint and humility when his ideas over and over again are rejected by nature before he arrives at one to *please her*. When the scientist does finally find such an idea, there is something very intimate in his feeling of communion with nature" (the italics are mine).

When the nonscientist understands what Mulliken meant when he talked of "pleasing nature," he will be on his way to understanding the scientific mind. He will realize what the pure scientist means when he talks of a "beautiful equation"—the statement of an idea in artistic form with an economy of means. We "please nature" when we search for, find, and *feel* beauty. It is as simple as that, yet it is not simply attained and maintained in a world where the marketplace dominates.

3. The beauty of the artifact: man's aspiration to create beautiful things. When we come to the beauty of the artifact—man's inspiration to produce with his own hands something of the quality that he has observed in his natural surroundings—we are in a complex and baffling domain. Much we must guess. A Paleolithic artist incised on the wall of a cave at Altamira the figure of a running deer. The draftsmanship, resulting from the acute observation of this prehistoric man, is by modern standards a beautiful thing. But did he intend beauty, or was it a propitiation of the spirit of the chase—a magical device to procure meat, and therefore a matter of utility? We cannot know: surely there is no harm in concluding that it could have been both. I have held in my hand the bowl of a ceremonial pipe, made of the red Catlinite claystone that came from southwestern Minnesota, but taken from a mound in northern Mississippi, the work of one of our prehistoric Indian artists. It is the figure of a man sitting and thinking—a forerunner of the famous Rodin sculpture, and not a whit less impressive. Did this early artist intend beauty? I think he did; though there may have been religious significance.

But clearly we are here in a region of taste, tradition, changing standards of judgment. The interpreter of the story of the artifact is not dealing with beauty as such, but with man's attitude toward beauty; and this can be made warmly appealing, for it is an appeal to the heart even more than to the mind. The standards of judgment in architecture change. The filigree gingerbread of the Victorian period is today a matter of mild amusement. Structures that were considered beautiful in their time cause pained surprise now. Yet, worldwide, there are not many people who do not thrill at the classic beauty of the Parthenon, the Maison Carré at Nîmes, or the Lincoln Memorial in Washington, D.C. And all of us are sensitive to harmony of structure and environment. The humble adobe dwelling arising from our southwestern desert, created from the desert soil itself and roofed with rush or with tiles shaped on the thigh of the builder, violates no principle of art. The most expensive structure, of architectural merit in itself, but alien to its environment, may be an excrescence—almost an ugliness. Hence the fine current effort around Washington, D.C., to procure scenic easements. The objection is not so much to the artifacts themselves: in relation to the greater natural beauty they may be in the wrong place.

One could go on endlessly in a discussion of the opportunity for the interpretation of man's aspiration to produce beautiful objects. More to the point at the moment is the effort to restore some of the natural beauty we have blighted, and to make resurgent an innate delight in the beauty of our environment: the aim of the program of beautification to which the wife of the president has given her enthusiasm and the prestige of her position.

As the interpreter, in or out of the National Park Service, is not needed to define or explain scenic beauty, neither does its opposite require interpretation. When Alice was in Wonderland, the Mock Turtle told her that he went to school with an old turtle who taught Uglification.

"I never heard of 'Uglification,'" Alice ventured to say. The Gryphon lifted up both its paws in surprise.

"Never heard of uglifying?" it exclaimed. "You know what to beautify is, I suppose?"

"Yes," said Alice, doubtfully. "It means to make anything prettier."

"Well, then," the Gryphon went on, "if you don't know what to uglify is, you *are* a simpleton."

Well we know what ugliness is, and the processes that create it. In the haste to gain material welfare we have forgotten, or chosen to forget; and the bill has now come due. To live willingly in tawdry surroundings is to become numb to their baleful influence upon us; they tend to seem as inevitable as climate. It is not so. It is already proved, in city, state, county, and town, that the feeling for beauty can be dramatized and renewed by *beautifying*. The start has been made.

What interpreters can do is to communicate, from their own conviction, *by indirection but with warmth*, this appeal to an always receptive human heart.

4. The beauty of human conduct, or behavior, of which man has shown himself capable. In the interpretation of the beauty of conduct of which the human being is capable, we come under the leering squint of the pessimist. We read in Emerson that "the beauty of nature must always seem unreal and mocking, until the landscape has human figures that are as good as itself."

"Perhaps," replies the cynic, "but tell me just when that will be."

We do have to go back to antiquity—to Socrates, Jesus, or the Roman general Regulus, for the answer to that. It is here and now, just as it was yesterday and the day before. The National Park System includes scores of historic memorials, the truest interpretation of which is the evidence that our country has possessed men and women of great moral beauty. And for each one of those a myriad of the humbler unknowns has lived and passed. The birthplace of Washington; the several areas that keep in memory the greatheartedness of Lincoln; the house at Appomattox, Virginia, where Grant and Lee revealed beautiful magnanimity on the one side and a nobility in the acceptance of defeat on the other; the farmer soldiers at the bridge in Concord, Massachusetts; an ample preservation of the Civil War battlefields—what are all these but the testimonials that man does transcend his animal boundary?

Recently in Vietnam, a soldier threw himself upon a hand grenade, saving the lives of his comrades. War is a terrible thing; the hope of mankind is that it will cease to be; yet it cannot be denied that out of its shambles have emerged valor and fortitude and self-sacrifice on the part of individual man and woman. William James, the Harvard philosopher, had this undeniable truth in mind when he wrote his "Moral Equivalent for War"—an attempt to find some other agent in life that would perform the same service to human character. That he failed is less important than that he showed his own beauty of conduct in the failure.

The interpreter in a monument or battlefield of war may thrill his hearer with the account of the mass action; the losses and gains in a swaying conflict; the skill of leadership. This can be made dramatic stuff, exciting the imagination, a capsuled fragment of the national past that must not be forgotten. But these things are an appeal to the mind, to logic and imagination. The appeal to the heart is the story of how in such tragic environment the human being finds the path to beauty of behavior.

V

The appeal for a renaissance of the appreciation of beauty—in the abstract and in its particular aspects—must not be allowed to falter. It is vital to our moral growth. It is a program of education. Perhaps it is truer to say that it is a program of reeducation, for we have always known, in our innermost recesses, our dependence upon beauty for the courage to face the problems of life. We have let ourselves forget. It is the duty of the interpreter to jog our memories.

Part III

Freeman Tilden's Later Interpretive Writings

CHAPTER 16

🔥 Mindsight
The Aim of Interpretation

*In this essay, Tilden presents to an environmentally savvy lay
audience what interpreters try to instill in the minds of visitors. In
doing so he defines interpretation and introduces some of the basic
interpretive concepts that he developed so eloquently and more fully
in* Interpreting Our Heritage.

*But in summoning forth the words of Charles Darwin—that "we
must see with the eye of the mind"—Tilden does more: he introduces
a concept that he terms "mindsight." The interpreter's task, he
suggests, is to plant the "seed of provocation" and help the visitor
see beyond the mind's eye. While the interpreter will probably never
know the harvest of the seed of provocation sown, Tilden states,
one "need not worry about that," provided that the interpreter "has
demonstrated that the beauty that lies behind what the eye sees is
far greater than that which is so seen."*

In Ralph Waldo Emerson's day, every well-to-do Bostonian looked
forward to what was called "the grand tour" of Europe. To such friends,
on their departure, the sage of Concord gave his affectionate blessing
and Godspeed. But he noted in his journal that they were not likely
to bring back anything of great value that they did not take abroad
with them. Henry David Thoreau echoed the philosophy when he remarked that the whole world was in Concord. All disappointments in
our use of leisure time arise from this blunt truism.

In this view, it must have been that when Charles M. Goethe of
Sacramento, California, visited Switzerland early in this century, he
carried with him plenty of perceptive eagerness. In one of the alpine
cantons he observed a pleasurable educational activity that he had
never seen practiced in his own country. Here were groups of tour-

Source: Freeman Tilden, "Mindsight: The Aim of Interpretation," *National Parks* 43, no. 260 (May 1969), 9–12. Reprinted with permission of *National Parks* magazine; © 1969 by National Parks Conservation Association.

ists being led upon nature walks by informed guides, learning at firsthand, on the very scene, the intricate web of plant and animal existence and the relationship of disparate names and facts. And the tourists seemed to be enjoying the adventure hugely. If this could be profitable fun in Switzerland, Goethe reasoned, why not in California? Back home, he interested some resort owners at Falling Leaf Lodge in Lake Tahoe in the idea. It worked. Vacationers found in this open-air learning something that paid unexpected dividends from holiday.

"Steve" Mather, the restless, innovating first director of the young National Park Service, was not tardy in hearing about the success at Lake Tahoe. He saw and heard; and he said, "We must have something like this at Yosemite!" So to Yosemite the practice went. It was "interpretation," though perhaps not so called at the outset. In its first season at Yosemite the program, conducted by Harold Bryant and Lloye Miller, drew 1,381 adults and children to the field trips and 25,732 to the campfire lectures. Meager numbers, indeed, when compared with the millions who can find these services available to them in the great park system of today: but it was testimony to the validity of the idea. The parks, enjoyable and inspiriting from many points of view, had found their highest-quality use—encouragement of our understanding of our place in nature, and among our fellow human beings.

Backed by a grant from the Laura Spelman Rockefeller Fund early in the 1920s, a group of educators, of which the naturalist Ansel F. Hall was field secretary, made the rounds of the then existing national parks and laid down a program of interpretation that has formed the basis of the effort ever since. Great names in the educational world were these: Hermon Bumpus, John C. Merriam, Wallace Atwood, Vernon Kellogg, Frank Oastler, and many other devoted teachers who were convinced that classroom instruction was made truly effective when it could be supplemented in the field *where the things were*.

Admittedly, the first efforts in interpretive work fumbled a bit. On the part of the educators perhaps there was a professional stiffness. If so, this was also rather sadly balanced by well-intentioned efforts to give entertainment. Indeed, some of the horseplay at Yellowstone campfires, encouraged by Mather himself, would give the present-day interpreter the shivers. But the activity was young and experimenting: and even at this moment the aspiring interpreter sometimes fails to realize that while entertainment is not a proper end of the art, yet the opposite of presenting his material in an entertaining manner is—simply being dull.

Precisely what is this thing called interpretation, which is now offered so extensively not only by the National Park Service but in many state parks, municipal and county areas, and city nature centers as well as in privately administered museums and historic sites? It would be easier to state precisely what it is not. It is not instruction. It is not avowed information, though it carries information with it. It is not forced upon anyone. Take it or leave it. If one takes it, one has it in many forms, the ideal being to make each form as attractive as possible—the guided trip, the marked trail, the campfire gathering, the slide talk, the motion picture, the exhibits and printed matter.

A somewhat clumsy but generally accepted definition in the "trade" is this: *an educational activity which aims to reveal meanings and relationships through the use of original objects, by firsthand experience and by illustrative media, rather than simply to communicate factual information.* If that sounds stuffy, you may call it "an attempt to reveal the truths that lie behind the appearances."

Human beings tend to do their wondering about the unusual. It is only when they begin to wonder about the usual that they begin to feel a harmony with the natural environment, or even with their own social existence. In that sense, the spectacular may even be the enemy of understanding. The transcendent earth forms seen in the primitive national parks, aesthetically joy giving and humbling as they are, are still not so truly awe inspiring as the miraculous factory contained in a blade of grass. The interpreter tries to lure the vacationer to become *pleasurably thoughtful* about this kind of beauty, instead of being content with looking and restlessly moving on. And considering how backward we are in learning the wise use of leisure time, his effort seems remarkably successful. Witness the grateful letters that flow into park service headquarters each year from those visitors who feel that interpretation has enlarged their vision and brightened their holiday.

There is no better example of the need for interpretation in the national parks than the great nearly tropical wilderness of Everglades. To the biologist it is a wonderland where the opportunity for research into its complex relationships never seems to end. Here the generative powers of sun and water create a food chain whose delicacy of balance is not to be found elsewhere on this continent. It has beauty; but not the kind that announces its presence in bold terms. Except for such transient sights as the nesting of the birds in Cuthbert Lake Rookery (which is not seen by most of the visitors to the park) and the gorgeous sunsets witnessed by those who remain in the park till evening, there is little that we call "spectacular." A flat, flat land, only a few feet above sea level at the highest point; vast expanses of saw grass bending with the breeze; even desolate acres of gaunt trees that were whipped to death and smothered by hurricane fury—this destructive visitation being as normal to the region as the erosion of a riverbed or a rockslide in the mountains—a glimpse of the relatively small number of alligators that persistent poaching has left alive. Or, by unlikely chance, a cougar could cross the highway; another of our vanishing species, and these are the remnants of a population that once flourished east of the Mississippi. "I don't see much in this park," says many a visitor who drives from the entrance station to Flamingo; even one who takes the trouble to make the short spur-trips that lead to points of special interest. Not much to see. No; truly, if one thinks of "sights" that startle, overwhelm, grasp with intensity. Even so, if the visitor could look with the sharp apprehension of the naturalist, there is much to "see." That, of course, is not to be expected.

Now comes upon the scene the interpreter, to reveal the beautiful truths that lie behind the appearances. Since the early days of interpretation, we have multiplied and refined many times the devices that one employs. But basically the principles upon which the interpreter works are unchanged. One must love the work and the subject, and one must like the people. Not necessarily persons: some of these vacationers are deplorable specimens. No; people. One must ever be learning while teaching. Patient; enthusiastic. The interpreter sees the vital importance of relating the subject of this discourse to something within the knowledge, the experience, and the ideals of his or her group. The interpreter will not belabor the subject matter. Often a single spark will set the desirable fire. Nor should the interpreter forget, in one's enthusiasm to teach the story of nature and humankind, that the basic need is to make clear the reasons why we have parks at all.

The good interpreter will have developed a philosophy about life, and about human needs, of his or her own. It will be frail, gauzy, since there is so much that nobody knows, and perhaps can ever know. The interpreter will not detail his or her philosophy. It will be implicit in what is said and by one's attitude. The job is very little to instruct, but rather to provoke the desire to know. One plants this seed of provocation, and will not know the harvest, nor need worry about that, if it be that one has demonstrated that the beauty that lies behind what the eye sees is far greater than that which is so seen.

One thing is sure, and must be underlined: that what one sees with the eyes is not enough for the attainment of understanding, either of the natural world or the social world of man. As Charles Darwin said, "We must see with the eye of the mind." Interpretation, whether in the National Park System or in any other place where it is offered, promotes that mindsight.

CHAPTER 17 🌿 That Elderly Schoolma'am
Nature

Long before the National Park Service and other federal, state, municipal, and private-sector parks and heritage sites began providing interpretation targeted to what has been termed "special populations" (such as the physically disabled, the young, foreign visitors, and seniors), Tilden recognized that site interpretation had to be made accessible to all visitors. In this essay, he poignantly shows how a naturalist was able to convey to a blind man the magnificence of Crater Lake.

Tilden suggests that "we are all of us somewhat blind, even those who believe their eyesight is faultless," and that "when it comes to understanding the why and the how of what we do manage to see, which is vital to a feeling of its reality, we all need what help we can get." After all, states Tilden, the interpreter's duty is not merely to point out something for visitors to look at, but rather to give them something to wonder about.

It happened at Crater Lake National Park, in Oregon.

Just inside the rim of the crater stands the Sinnott Memorial Observation Station, cunningly ensconced so as to give visitors the best possible view of the lake and its surroundings, which suggests the origin and subsequent geologic story of the region. And to make understanding as easy as possible, the memorial is equipped with exhibits, field glasses fixed upon key points, and a large relief map.

On this relief model, with a scale of one foot to six miles, are depicted the prominent features of the landscape—Wizard Island, the Phantom Ship, the deep glacial valleys, and other important land-

Source: Freeman Tilden, *The National Parks*, revised by Paul Schullery. © 1951 Alfred A. Knopf, Inc.; copyright renewed 1979 by Freeman Tilden; © 1986 Paul Schullery. Used by permission of Alfred A. Knopf, a division of Random House, Inc.

forms that are part of one of the finest of our preserved natural wonders.

One day in summer the park naturalist, just then inside the memorial, was introduced to a man of middle age whose appearance at once whispered: "Here is a man who is different." It was not his clothes, though he was fastidiously dressed. It was not his face, though the face lighted up with fine intelligence at the introduction. But there was something about the gloved hands, the walking stick hung by a curved handle on his arm, something about the erectness of his posture, the grip of his hand, that set the naturalist wondering. A pair of very dark glasses that the man wore forced the conclusion that the man was totally blind.

Blindness was not mentioned; it did not need to be. But when the visitor asked gently, "Will you describe Crater Lake to me?" the naturalist knew that he had a task before him. This man had come to *see* Crater Lake. Perhaps his friends back home had vainly tried to describe it to him; now he was here to see it for himself.

The poignancy of the situation gave a tug at the heart of the naturalist. How to convey to a blind man the distances, the heights, the highlights and reflections, and the forests on the crater walls—to say nothing of that blue of the water that has no counterpart? For even we who have our normal sight fall far short of full appreciation of this picture—we see only in part and understand only in part.

The naturalist had an inspiration. Perhaps, after all, he could make his visitor see what he wished. He knew that with the blind the other senses usually become compensatingly acute. He knew, too, that the Danish poet Henrik Hertz was voicing no sentimental illusion when he wrote, in his *King René's Daughter*:

In the material eye, you think, sight lodges!
The eye is but an organ. Seeing streams
From the soul's inmost depths. The fine, perceptive nerve
Springs from the brain's mysterious workshop.

He knew that this is just a simple truth, demonstrated every day in his experience: for every park naturalist observes that of the millions of visitors with reasonably normal eyes, there are all grades of sight, from seeing astonishingly much to seeing not much at all.

"I think I can show you Crater Lake, sir," said the naturalist, "if you will take off your gloves and put your hands in mine."

The gloves came off.

As the naturalist told me: "I took his hands and moved them around the crater model in relief, trying to convey through his sensitive fingertips and through his quick, eager mental perception the general shape of the crater and the variations of its rim skyline. By putting his thumb tips together, with hands extended, the little fingers accomplished the scaled diameter of the lake.

"I asked him if he had an idea of distances. He said that he could relate distances to those he experienced in walking. It was obvious that when he knew the scale spanned by his hands, he could sense the great expanse covered by the crater and its water.

"Then we moved the fingertips up the modeled face of Llao Rock, the two inches on the model representing the sheer face of almost twenty-two hundred feet of drop. He understood that there were two thousand more feet of the crater below the surface of the water. His fingers told him the conical shape of Wizard Island. The tiny depression at the summit of the cone gave him not only that special feature, but the type of many other craters too. He could see, through his fingers, the lava flows that extend from the base of the island cone. And then we traced out the U-shaped glacial valleys and compared them with the V-shaped stream-cut valleys in other parts of the park. Then, with a model block, I could explain to him that perhaps—we do not certainly know—this whole mountain peak, where now the crater and lake exist, was another of the great volcanic cones that rise along this long mountain uplift—not unlike Mount Hood, Mount Rainier, and others—but that this one suffered a strange collapse. It was so evident that he saw it all.

"But then, as we finally must, we came to the great outstanding quality of Crater Lake—its color. How encompass that? How convey the importance of the reflection of the sky, the action of the wind, the refracted sunlight, and all those known and unknown factors which result in this blue to end all blues? And how suggest its crystal clearness?"

Suddenly the man said, with a little catch in his voice: "I do remember—I think—yes, I know I do remember something of the blue of the sky—when I was a little boy—it comes back to me now."

Well, the blue of Crater Lake is not that of the sky, of course. It is not the blue of anything—except Crater Lake. But *blue* he could recollect, and perhaps in that "mysterious workshop of the brain" he charted the color better than the naturalist could possibly know.

"He thanked me and was led away," said the naturalist. "He went away with a smile on his face. And I shall not forget that smile. He had not only seen Crater Lake. He had extended his power of seeing—which was an achievement beyond price."

Well, we are all of us somewhat blind, even those who believe their eyesight is faultless. In viewing natural objects and scenes, the total amount we discern is nearly nothing compared with what there is to see. Even the trained naturalist, whose business it is to make the fullest use of his senses, will readily admit that he is living a life of constant discovery. And when it comes to understanding the why and the how of what we do manage to see, which is vital to a feeling of its reality, we all need what help we can get.

The National Park Service had scarcely come into existence before the need was felt for a program of interpretation. It can be called, and correctly enough, an educational program, but to call it so is to invite a misunderstanding of its true purposes. Very few persons visit the national parks to study. They do not want to take a course in botany or geology. They want to look at the spectacular displays, the flowers, the birds, the wild creatures; they want to idle, browse, inhale deeply, hike, go horseback riding, take pictures, mingle with folks doing all these things, and forget their jobs or their routine existence.

That is all they want. Rather, that is all they think, at first, they want. But almost all of them find that it is not enough. They see the eruption of the Old Faithful geyser at Yellowstone; or in early summer they watch the tremendous gush of water at Yosemite Falls; or at Mount Rainier they see the avalanche fawn lilies pursuing the retreating snowbanks. These things are no longer something just to look at; they are something to wonder about. The birds and the flowers ask for a little intimacy. Nature holds out a hand. There are few who do not grasp it. There are secrets. There are few who do not want to penetrate some of them.

Good books about nature, and descriptive of places and things few of us can hope to visit, are precious, and we should feel poor without them. But at best, if it remains a matter of reading or of pictures, the acquaintance is secondhand. In the national parks, whoever wishes it can greet these things in their homes; it is firsthand. Nature is the teacher; the classroom is outdoors; the textbooks are the very things you see. And what the interpreters of the National Park Service really do is arrange an introduction to the schoolma'am and lead visitors to the place where class is in session.

The great fun is in seeing everything "in place." Mr. Squeers, master of Dotheboys Hall in Dickens's *Nicholas Nickleby*, was a cruel, bullying, cowardly rascal; but I have always thought that his explanation of his teaching method, while selfish, had great merit. He said that he taught the boys to spell *winder* w-i-n-d-e-r, and then go and wash it! To see a natural wonder "in place," in its surroundings, with the bright sky overhead and the mountains over yonder and the good earth underfoot—that is something that cannot be had from books.

All over the western country, you are likely to come upon bits of petrified wood—not of the gorgeous hues of the logs in Petrified Forest National Park, but easily identifiable as fragments of trees that once grew in places perhaps now desert, but formerly inundated by some invading sea. One day I toiled several miles up a sweltering dry creek bed just to have a look at the stump of a petrified tree of which I had been told. It was not much to look at. What had been the trunk was hardly more than a foot above the ground, and even that part was badly broken. But the roots of the tree were there. It was *in place*. That was the very spot where it had actually sprouted, grown, and later been overwhelmed. I felt rewarded. It was a thrill. No vagrant chips could satisfy like that.

In some such way the interpretive work in the parks carries on its policy of introducing visitors to the schoolma'am, the original teacher. By means of guided trips, in the company of a naturalist ranger; by the creation of nature trails, so selected and labeled that visitors may go exploring by themselves; by campfire talks, observation stations, museums, and other devices, visitors to the parks may take as much as they please of the opportunities to observe and learn. In this school there are no marks, no examination papers.

To go on a walking trip with a naturalist guide, or better still to make a three-day trip on horses into the backcountry not accessible except in this manner, is to have an enthusiast for a companion. These naturalist rangers are all-around people. They must be resourceful, tactful, patient, and understanding. If the blind man who was shown the crater of ancient Mount Mazama had happened to be on the trail with a naturalist, he would have found that sight, however precious, is not the only desirable sense, for the guide would have made plants come to keen perception by their odors and tastes; trees by the feeling of their bark; birds by their call notes and songs. Even many rocks can be recognized, or guessed, by touch, especially when one knows the kind of rocks that might be expected to occur in a locality.

Many visitors to the parks prefer to wander and inspect alone or with a companion or two. For these the "self-guiding nature trails" have been created. These paths find their way along objects or to places that the average visitor is most likely to wish to see, and the labeled rocks or plants or trees answer the questions the stroller would ask a guide if one were present. They indicate, too, such features as the superb polish and striations made by the glaciers of Yosemite, or the former locations of the retreating Nisqually Glacier at Mount Rainier National Park. All the major parks have these self-guiding trails. They will never quite take the place of a guide. Animals and birds, for instance, cannot be labeled, and naturally it is impossible to identify any but salient features. But for those who dislike to join larger parties, the self-guiding nature trails are admirable.

Who can forget the campfire talks in the high country, when the blaze from burning logs sends flittering gleams and stalking shadows into the branches of the surrounding trees, and the night air has just the amount of invigorating nip to put an edge on the appetite for this wilderness experience? The setting is perfect; and here is a ranger who talks from no schoolbook study, but from a rich experience with the forests, the birds and other animals, the upland streams and fish, and the threading canyons. They are informal, these naturalist talks, but they have meat in them. They are chat, but never chatter. They call for questions from the audience, and the questions seldom fail to come. Visitors who gather round some of these campfires in the larger places are not numbered in the hundreds but in the thousands. The talks are given not only in the campgrounds, but in the hotels, lodges, and museums.

Finally, to supply the information that will make a visit to the parks and monuments the fullest possible experience, there are museums and observation stations.

The observation stations are just what the name implies, but they may also have something of the quality of museums. The station at Yavapai Point, on the south rim of the Grand Canyon, one of the first to be erected, was the result of the most careful study. In a very real sense the whole of Grand Canyon is a museum, and so is every other park and monument. Likewise any point where you happen to be is an observation point. But for those who believe they have neither the time nor the inclination to explore the details of the canyon, the observation station at Yavapai seems to be almost ideal.

First you have a glimpse of the wide range of the great chasm and that first shock of its vastness. Then you may go out upon the parapet at Yavapai and look through the telescopes for closer views of points of special interest. Through one telescope the rushing, muddy Colorado River can be seen; through another the top of Cedar Mountain; and still others show the differences in the rock structure of the walls. At hand are references to these very details. Here is a sample of the silty river water—you may see how enormous is the quantity of land material being poured toward the Gulf of California. Here now is a "formation column." You have seen these formations through the glass; now they are at your fingertips, in the shape of actual slabs of rock from the canyon walls. Here is a "fossil column," which reveals the evidences of life still remaining in those stratified cliffs. And here are several large sandstone slabs sowing the footprints of animals, reptiles, and land—water forms that ages ago crept along on the plastic surface that at that time—but only at that time—was the level of the land hereabouts. It will be more of an adventure, certainly, if visitors go down into the canyon and see similar footprints where these animals crawled along, on the very spot—the thing *in place*—but if not, then these sandstone fragments are the next best thing.

Museums anywhere, everywhere, are a problem. The museums of the National Park Service, those of the wilderness areas and those of the historical classifications, are without doubt the finest of their kind in the world. Into them has gone superior intelligence, taste, painstaking accuracy, superb craftsmanship, and, indeed, art.

Much as they are used, and as really popular as they are, the museums of Yellowstone, Yosemite, Rocky Mountain, Lassen, and the other wilderness parks and monuments should have even more visitors than they do. It is not expected that everyone who visits the parks will go to the museums. Not all who visit the parks even see the major features. I know of one man who went in by the Cody Gate of Yellowstone, spent two weeks in camp at Fishing Bridge, and saw nothing but that locality. He was well and happy all the time and he said he had had a great vacation.

There is, however, such a thing as "public resistance" to museums of any kind, and it has been a source of discussion not only in this country but in Europe as well. It has even been suggested that the name "museum" be changed to something else; and although this may sound absurd, you have to consider that the naturalists are aiming at telling the story of the parks to the greatest possible number, and the end to be achieved is the finest pleasure of the public and the noblest uses of the parks. The name is unimportant.

I understand well why some people dodge museums, especially if they have visited unfortunate samples. I have been through historical society museums that left me dazed and dizzy. Each article displayed was valuable in its way, and possibly a treasure, but the whole setup was inchoate. It is really bewildering to find a letter from Napoleon to Josephine reposing beside a stuffed albino squirrel. If you add to those a fireman's hat just above a first edition of James Fenimore Cooper, and both of these in front of a Revolutionary musket, the display becomes almost crushing.

You will not find museums of the National Park Service of that kind. They limit themselves to what is local, coherent, important, and authentic. They tell a story, and having told *that* story, they stop. They tell the story in a way that requires no special knowledge to understand. Because they are the work of enthusiastic experts and artists, they stimulate the imagination without diffusion. They amplify many confidences that nature makes in low whispers.

CHAPTER 18 🔥 The Constructive
Aspect of Inaction

*Like any skilled interpreter, Tilden was well read and often drew
inspiration from the books and authors he liked most. Ralph Waldo
Emerson, for example, was among his favorites. In this essay, Tilden
reflects on words that Plato uttered some 2,500 years ago, when the
Greek philosopher stated that "not-being is a state of being."*

*At first, Tilden thought these words seemed to have little if
anything to do with interpretation. Then, once he stopped thinking
too hard about it, he made an intellectual breakthrough: "If
not-being is a state of being, then it follows that not-doing is
a state of doing." The ramifications for interpreters suddenly
became clear. Interpreters are occasionally—"providentially," he
declared—"protected by your inaction." This became the theme of a
presentation first delivered at the annual meeting of the Association
of Interpretive Naturalists in Cumberland Falls, Kentucky, on April
10, 1965. It was subsequently presented from time to time in a
slightly revised form at the Mather Training Center in Harpers Ferry.*

*Those who were privileged to hear Tilden deliver a presentation
were always in for a good show; but when he delivered a talk
accompanied by a few well-selected slides, listeners were in for a real
treat. Attendees long remembered the brilliant luster of this witty,
thought-provoking talk. In its printed form the spark of Tilden's
personal appearance may be lacking, but the words he spoke and the
message he conveyed is nonetheless profound and important.*

My good friends, I salute you all.

When I deliver a discourse, which is nowadays not often, I attend
strictly to business. I have no exordium of funny stories. Life is a serious matter, and becoming more perplexing all the time. So, to the
business at hand.

Source: National Park Service, *Trends* 2, no. 3 (July 1965): 21–24. Reprinted
with permission of the National Park Service.

I did have the idea, in connection with this important exposition, to indulge in a slight innovation. This was going to consist of showing three slides at the very beginning of my paper, and then having some more slides at the end. Nobody ever did anything like that. But when I considered the plan, I saw two objections. I had waited till it was too late to get hold of the slides I wanted, or to have them produced. And then I could see a certain disadvantage that might come, before a speaker has established the interest of his listeners, in having any prolonged dark period.

I shall therefore indicate on the screen the three slides that you would see if I had not abstained from showing them. I think I can make them very real to you.

The first slide that you are not seeing here is a squirrel. Any kind of squirrel. *Sciurus Carolinensis* will do. The second slide I do not have with me is a picture of a snail. In this case, an African snail. *Achatina fulica*. The third picture that does not appear here is merely the mathematical symbol—the square root of minus one. You might well become alarmed at this point on my behalf. I assure you something good will come of it.

I shall deal first with the squirrel.

Many years ago, I became a member of an actor's club in New York. I was writing for the stage then. The first close acquaintance I made in the Players was Guy Nichols, a charming man who should have been a naturalist. He loved the woods, he knew the birds, he was a pioneer organic gardener. He was not a distinguished actor. He was what we called, in the profession, a "ham." But he hammed efficiently. His wife, a handsome lady of unpredictable disposition, was an actress—of minor talent, not a leading lady.

I suppose she was what we could call a "hamlet."

Guy was normally a temperate man. He did, on being sufficiently provoked by life, take a few calming drinks, and those naturally led to other drinks. Mrs. Nichols frowned upon this sort of tranquilizer. At the time my anecdote begins, both Guy and Hazel were with a road show, playing one-week stands across the country. They were traveling in a specially chartered Pullman—the old kind that had a drawing room in one end, and the rest were sections, upper and lower. Guy and Hazel had number-one section, which would be the first on the left when you entered the door. Therefore it was over the wheels.

Guy and his wife were not, at the moment, on speaking terms. Guy had been behaving badly. At the moment, as the train rolled on, Guy was still not sober. It was an unpleasant situation. It is *very* embarrassing to spend the night in a hotel room with a lady with whom you are not on speaking terms. In a Pullman section it should be nothing less than tragic. Over the wheels.

The train stopped to let off a few passengers, or to take water for the engine, and Guy got out on the platform and hoped something would happen.

It did.

A boy with freckles and some front teeth missing came up to him, holding something under his jacket. He said "Mither, do you wanna buy a swthquirrel?"

There is this much about alcohol: it is the great affirmative agent. Alcohol, as some of my readers may know, says "yes," whereas branch water, or well water, even with chlorine, tends to say, "It sounds attractive, defer your decision." This was a great opportunity for Guy to test the virtues of inaction. Guy should have said: "I will not act precipitately. I shall consider this purchase of a squirrel. I shall get into this chair car just ahead of our Pullman and ruminate on this matter." By the time Guy had so revolved the opportunity, the train would have moved several miles from the station.

But Guy did not use this opportunity for inaction. Instead, he said: "How much?" The answer was: "Fifty thents." Guy said to himself, "This is my opportunity. Maybe Hazel has always wanted a squirrel. Maybe a squirrel has great significance in Freudian psychology. She will greatly appreciate my thoughtfulness. This will effect reconciliation."

The train whistle blew, and Guy leaped up the steps. He had got out on the platform with a problem. Now he had a squirrel. In his pocket!

I think you see this coming. Yes, just as you are thinking (you wouldn't have it otherwise), Guy opened the door of the Pullman where his wife was gloomily knitting—a shroud, or something—and cried, exultingly, "Here is something I bought for you, Darling." So saying, he threw the squirrel into her lap. Naturally the squirrel sank its teeth into her lily white hand. Mrs. Nichols ran down the aisle screaming that her husband had hired a wild animal to give her hydrophobia . . .

Needless to say, the reconciliation was delayed. There is a moral here. I shall now pass quickly to the African snail.

We are now to visit Micronesia, that galaxy of small islands. East of the Philippine Sea and northeast of New Guinea.

Before World War I the inhabitants of these islands, who raised chickens and pigs and garden vegetables, and received coconuts as a bonus from nature, were afflicted with two scourges—rats, which had come ashore from visiting ships, and African snails, which had been imported under the hallucination that they were good to eat. The rats were feeding on the poultry and the snails were eating up the vegetation.

Let me briefly describe the giant African snail. It is a foot long. It is *not* a foodstuff. It has the peculiar properties that the longer it is boiled the tougher it gets and the worse it stinks. There were prisoners of war in the islands during World War II who preferred to starve to death. I am told that a hopeful Japanese canned several hundred packages with the Japanese market in view. At last report, being a frugal man, he was eating the remaining three dozen cans himself, but without enthusiasm.

But that's aside. The *action* story I am offering you deals with the homemade, or do-it-yourself efforts to eradicate pests.

Pure inspiration.

In all this, I must make clear, the professional biologist is innocent. He was never once consulted.

First, someone had heard that in the Japanese zoos the giant monitor lizard feeds avidly on rats. There's an idea! So now we introduce *Varanus* into the islands. But the lizard is a diurnal creature, and the rats are mainly nocturnal, so they never got well acquainted. But the lizard began to eat the eggs and the young chickens at a rate that made the rats jealous, and you have to remember, too, that the poultry had been doing their part in eating young snails.

But wait—now we have a better idea! How about *Bufo marinus*, the giant Central American toad? He would be the ideal enemy of snails, would he not?

Not!

The toad *Bufo marinus* does not hide in the daytime as effectively as rats, so the giant lizard fed on *Bufo*. Ah—but also the toads have potent poison glands in their skin, which sometimes proved fatal to lizards, and even more often to the pigs, for they caught young toads and died, and so did the cats and dogs that after all were the chief eradicators of rats.

And so—but I need not proceed further with this. There is much more of it. It goes round and round. But you get the drift, I think. When the islanders were last consulted about it, they wept for the long-gone Golden Age when they had only rats and snails to deal with. In other words they had discovered something that I venture now—at this point—to call the Virtue of Not Doing Something. Or, the constructive aspect of INACTION.

I turn now to the third and last of the nonexistent slides you are not seeing. This was merely planned to be a mathematical symbol— the square root of minus one.

There are many of you here who understand the use, in an equation, of this imaginary number. I do not; and I would rather not have it explained to me, if you please. I have a purely metaphysical notion of this symbol, which is such a source of satisfaction to me that I don't want it disturbed.

To me, then, this symbol represents what Plato was thinking of when, 2,500 years ago, he said that not-being is a state of being. *Not-being is a state of being.*

At first I could make nothing of that. But as soon as I quit thinking too hard about it, it became clear. And if not-being is a state of being, then it follows that not-doing is a state of doing. Your whole life, to make a practical application of the idea, has constantly been directed as much by what you have not done, as by what you have done. I merely point out the common regret, "If I had only done so and so." I think you will find, too, that looking back over your own experience, the source of your chagrins was oftener what you did than what you did not. Occasionally, you were providentially protected by your inaction.

I would go so far as to say that, in the field of preservation, whether of natural beauty or man-made structures—granted that once the act is effected of setting them aside from spoliation—the basic policy of administration must be that of either doing nothing, or doing the least possible required to preserve. You preserve mainly by inaction. I expect to give you some examples a little later.

You might at this point raise the reasonable objection that a world of inaction would be a world of stagnation. My reply to that is that you need not worry. *Homo sapiens* is an animal that craves to be doing something—usually something unwise; which will result in doing something else even less wise. I do not expect to muster a great multitude of followers of my gospel. There's no fun in not doing something. To see something that would move if you pushed it and not to give it a shove requires great restraint. Don't worry. You will always find enough people who want to act, at least plenty of people who want you to do something about something, so that there will be no atrophy.

Consider the case of dropping the atomic bombs on the Japanese. Whether this was wise or unwise, ethical or unethical, I make no judgment. But nobody can doubt that if the decision had been *not* to drop them, it might have vastly affected the future of the world. Would this have been constructive inaction? I leave it to you—and to the future.

I am now ready to proceed with my slides. I hope they are here. Yes, they are here.

It seems safe now to have a period of darkness in the room.

My first slide is an organizational chart.

I have always wanted to make a chart about something, but I never saw a good opportunity. I should like to make a graph, too, but I'm not sure what it would show. It is difficult to make a graph when you are operating on a plateau. I settle for a chart.

You will understand, please, that this chart depicts a purely hypothetical agency. I don't think we need any more actual agencies at present. I suggest merely an orderly way in which inaction could take form, and proceed.

Look first at the fountainhead. The Agency of Planned Inaction, as I style it, has nothing to do with mental laziness or what is sometimes called foot dragging. It would be headed by a discreet executive with a talent for not doing things, as a way of life. A man, you might say, never weary of not doing. He will set standards for taking inaction.

On one side you see the Branch of Tentative Negation. This branch will primarily be always ready to suggest the best method by which things should not be done. There are two offices contributory to this branch, as you see here. One of them deals with definite postponement, and the other with indefinite postponement.

On the other side, we have a Computer Branch. This is new, and responds to the steady increase of electronic help. The computer here will have all the absent parameters necessary for coming to no conclusion about anything. From this confusion naturally comes an overflow into the Section of Delayed Correspondence. By the way, I don't mean a *mild* confusion. That never helps. You need *utter* confusion.

We are now prepared to go on with my slides intended to show the constructive aspects of inaction.

This is a sand dune, on the Atlantic Coast, which was *not* bulldozed away to make room for a parking area. Result: in the great tides of September 1962, the ocean did *not* break in at this point and flood hundreds of summer cottages and hot dog emporia out of existence.

I show you the reverse side of this. Here you are looking out from the Castillo de San Marcos at St. Augustine, toward the inlet and the man-made channel through which the shrimp boats enter with their cargoes. To protect this channel from shoaling, jetties were built. That was good. But wait. Down the coast about five miles from here there is a place called St. Augustine Beach.

This was a fine gently sloping beach of white sand. There was a boardwalk here, and you went down three or four steps onto this beach. When I last saw it, there was a nine-foot jump, and the beach continues to disappear with every wild storm. The sea is cutting rapidly landward at this point. I need not elaborate.

This time a little map, because I couldn't get a picture that would illustrate. This is in Grand Teton.

Olaus Murie, in 1963, was describing somewhere with enthusiasm how you came up String Lake, then over a little rise of ground and lo—before you is the gem, Leigh Lake. Some people would like a road in, so that they could stay in their cars and ride up to the shore of Leigh Lake and say, "Ah-h-h." I indicate the place where the road has *not* been built.

This is inaction actually taking place:

Here is the surrender room at the McLean House at Appomattox, where Lee surrendered to Grant. Somebody proposed that it would be nice to have wax figures of Grant and Lee in this room. I point out the wax figures that are *not* there, due to planned inaction. This is wax Grant. This is wax Lee.

This is a mountain side in the southern Appalachians. I point out the place, approximately, where a ski lift has *not* been installed. A product of the Office of Indefinite Postponement.

Refer to my chart.

This is the south rim of the Grand Canyon. I point out the spot where a church, with a picture window, has *not* been erected. I avoid further comment. A touchy subject.

Finally, something nearer where we gather this evening.

Yes, Cumberland Falls—with its moonbow. There is not time here to tell the inspiriting story of the way these lovely falls were saved from the drowning of a hydroelectric power development. It was back in the Roaring Twenties. The power interests were amply financed and powerful. But Tom Wallace of the *Louisville Times* and the valiant preservation group in nearby Corbin saved the day. Read the tale of it someday and be heartened.

I merely point to the picture and say, "Hereabouts is where the dam was *not* built."

Those are my slides. I have a few final words, of a more intimate sort.

William Henry Jackson, the pioneer photographer and artist, when he was ninety-five, I think, said that he had often been asked for the secret of his longevity. He said he didn't really know, but he had recently seen a copy of a book entitled *Alcohol, the Friend of Man*. He thought the author had a point.

Well, that is not my case. I owe my longevity, I am sure, to two things: (1) The letters I have written and decided not to send; and (2) The clever things I started to say—and decided to abstain. It was my own personal view, you see, of the preservative quality of Planned Inaction.

CHAPTER 19

🌿 Two Concord Men in a Boat

Nature writers and interpreters share much in common. Both try to express feelings, thoughts, and emotions using words—written or spoken—that they hope will educate and at times move people to action. Tilden was a devotee of the transcendentalist authors who not only loved words but also were committed to making new demands on literature and on the reading public. Authors like Henry David Thoreau wrote metaphor-laden, personal, often prophetic essays, designed, as Thoreau said of his own Walden, *"to wake my neighbors up."*

Tilden was a newspaperman through and through, with a penchant for an easy-to-read style. Occasionally, though, he broke from the mode of writing he worked most comfortably in and dabbled in weightier prose. In this essay, Tilden did just that when he created an imaginary conversation between the two men who both influenced if not revolutionized environmental thinking—Ralph Waldo Emerson and his younger colleague Thoreau. In the end, Tilden concludes that the works and moral imperatives of both men today are "fruiting in the efforts of preservationists and interpreters everywhere."

"I go with my friend," wrote Ralph Waldo Emerson in one of his essays on nature, "to the shore of our little river, and with one stroke of the paddle I leave the village politics . . . and pass into a delicate realm of sunset and moonlight, too bright almost for spotted man to enter without novitiate and probation."

Who was this friend of Emerson's? Was it Henry David Thoreau? It is altogether likely. In that event, the paddling was done by the younger man—by him who built the cabin on Walden Pond and spent two years there with the ruffed grouse he called "my hens and chickens." It was not because the elder philosopher would have been

Source: Freeman Tilden, "Two Concord Men in a Boat," *Massachusetts Audubon* 50, no. 2 (1958): 78–82. Originally published by *National Parks* magazine; reprinted with permission of National Parks Conservation Association.

unwilling to lend a hand with the oar. Henry would simply have distrusted the sage's watermanship. He regarded Mr. Emerson with high respect and almost with affection. He could appreciate better than most readers the beauty and truth of the Emersonian meditations upon nature in the abstract. He had no illusions about his companion's dexterity in the use of tools.

In lecturing upon "Man the Reformer," Emerson perhaps surprised even himself with the discovery that "manual labor is the study of the external world." Then he added something that must have made Thoreau smile. "When I go into my garden with my spade, and dig a bed, I feel such an exhilaration and health, that I discover that I have been defrauding all this time in letting others do for me what I should have done with my own hands." Thoreau, who spent two years in the Emerson household as a sort of handyman-guest, had observed that it was only necessary for the sudden death of a pear tree that Mr. Emerson should spade up around it. Besides, the total Emerson spading in a hundred years would not have worn out a wooden implement. Yet there is no insincerity here. Emerson, paddling his literary canoe, bumped aground on a metaphor.

In moments of calmer examination, Mr. Emerson knew well that he was no tiller of Concord soil. "With brow bent, with firm intent, the pale scholar leaves his desk to draw a freer breath and get a juster statement of his thought in the garden walk. He stoops to pull up a purslain, or a dock, that is choking the young corn, and finds there are two: close behind the last is a third; he reaches out his hand to a fourth; behind that are four thousand and one. He is heated and untuned, and by-and-by, wakes up from his idiot dream of chickweed and redroot, to remember his morning thought, and to find that, with his adamantine purpose, he has been duped by a dandelion."

There you have it, in as delicate humor as ever was written. The "pale scholar" is Emerson himself. He is drolly viewing his own estrangement from the intimate contact with nature. He honestly prefers his meditation unmixed with vegetables. He declines to be "drugged by the smell of the plants." "The genius of reading and gardening are antagonistic," he says.

Even Thoreau, at Walden, admitted this much. "I did not read books the first summer: I hoed beans."

But there was a wide gulf here between the two men. Emerson, freed from weed pulling, wrote up his journal and composed an essay, and kept up with modern scientific advance. What did Thoreau do with this broad margin of leisure? "I sat in my sunny doorway from sunrise till noon, rapt in a revery . . . while the birds sang around, or flitted noiseless through the house."

This contentment to sit in the doorway and simply to let nature flow over him—no ambition even to make a practical use of the revery—was what Mr. Emerson could not understand about Henry. With all that obvious talent of his young friend, why didn't Thoreau affect something, instead of just being "captain of a huckleberry party"? He could be a capable civil engineer. Emerson confided this sentiment to his journal. Had he mentioned it to Henry, the reply would have been obvious. "My pressing engagements with nature, Mr. Emerson, leave me no time for such things. I had to spend the whole morning of this day trying to outmaneuver a loon on Walden pond." Besides, Thoreau had a deep suspicion of applied science. "Our inventions," he said, "are but improved means to an unimproved end." Had Henry foreseen such a device as an electric toothbrush, he never would have left Walden.

It was a time of what Emerson called "small, sour and fierce schemes," when these two men were moving along the sluggish current of the Concord River in their skiff. The schemes were mostly devoted toward getting rich quickly by exploiting the seemingly endless natural resources of a frontier. Already the primeval pines of northern Maine were about gone. Emerson was an investor in railroad shares, to discover later that this was not only one of those small and sour schemes, but disappointing, too. A visiting Frenchman of the period compared the feverish devastation of the American landscape to the ruin left by "an army on the march."

In general, these two men in the boat were in agreement. They were both, in their ways, trying to flag down the rush of materialism and to warn that any reckless plunder of nature leaves men inevitably sick and sorry. But one of them was a born naturalist, and the other, for want of a better term, we might call a humanist. And thus we see them, as they paddle along. Emerson sitting at the stern, eyes neither wholly open nor shut, conscious of a vague wealth of beauty around him; but Thoreau observing the wedge-form wake of a muskrat, the skating insects inshore, the shape and texture of leaves; nothing escapes those eyes. There is a bittern standing at the river edge, with his bill pointed upward questioningly. Mr. Emerson has been meditating on man's place in nature: the bittern escaped his notice.

Emerson could write, so beautifully and truly, "At the gates of the forest the surprised man of the world is forced to leave his city estimates of great and small, wise and foolish. The knapsack of custom falls off his back . . . here is a sanctity which shames our religions, and reality which discredits our heroes"—and so for two pages of lovely prose about man "nestling in nature," and "drawing his living . . . for her roots and grains." But when he wrote his poem "Each and All" we find Emerson indulging in a rhetorical figure that for Thoreau would have been unthinkable.

> I thought the sparrow's note from heaven,
> Singing at dawn on the alder bough;
> I brought him home, in his nest, at even;
> He sings his song, but it cheers not now,
> For I did not bring home the river and sky;—
> He sang to my ear,—they sang to my eye.

"Fine as the thought is, Mr. Emerson," Thoreau could have said, "here is a false note. You just cannot bring home a singing bird in his nest; and if you could, he wouldn't sing."

Similarly, Emerson has a tiny poem called simply "Fable." The mountain and the squirrel have a dispute in which the squirrel is jeered for his littleness. The animal retorts:

"If I cannot carry forests on my back, / Neither can you crack a nut."

Thoreau could have told Emerson that the word "crack" conveys an entirely wrong idea. He might have shown the sage a half-eaten hickory nut and pointed out how neatly the animal chisels a panel through the thinnest part of the shell, which is directly over the lobes of meat. Mr. Emerson was of course thinking of the way he cracked nuts, which probably with a hammer, and a flatiron held between his knees.

It seems a bit ungenerous to offer such objections where the poet's intent is so lofty; nor does it actually invalidate that intent; it only dilutes the total effect.

Though they had so much in common, as natural and moral

philosophers, there was one cardinal point on which Emerson and Thoreau never could have agreed. When the Walden dweller said, "I love the wild not less than the good," or "What man calls wildness is a civilization other than his own," or when he completely identified himself with nature in the simple words, "Morning is when I am awake and there is a dawn in me," Emerson shook his head. He would have replied: "In the divine order, intellect is primary; nature secondary." Or, "The beauty of nature must always seem unreal and lacking until the landscape has human figures that are as good as itself. If there were good men, there would never be this rapture in nature."

Bluntly put, Emerson feared nature. He was not physically afraid. He resented its competition with those high hopes he entertained for man. Once, he apologized for taking this position. "I have no hostility to nature, but a child's love to it. I expand and live in the warm day like corn and melons. . . . I do not wish to fling stones at my beautiful mother, nor soil my gentle next. I only wish to indicate the true position of nature in regard to man, wherein to establish man, all right education tends."

It is clear, as we read the extensive journals kept by these Concord thinkers, that each served as a whetstone for the other. They agreed far more than they disagreed as to ultimate truths. Intellectually, Emerson was as much nonconformist as Thoreau. The important point is that both of them sowed the seeds of an appraisal of nature that, though it took years to arrive, are today fruiting in the efforts of preservationists and interpreters everywhere.

In the mid-1950s, the National Park Service faced a crisis. In part because of other more pressing governmental priorities throughout World War II, in the postwar years the parks were deteriorating while visitation was mushrooming. Congress was failing to provide sufficient funds for operations, and of special concern to Tilden, "the public was not getting from the parks the services to which they are entitled and which they have shown they desire." Tilden felt strongly that the parks were "without that degree of protection and maintenance without which any such priceless preserves must ultimately be impaired or lost." In response to the crisis, NPS director Conrad Wirth devised a bold initiative.

MISSION 66 was a long-range rehabilitation program designed to catch the imagination of Americans—from the president and Congress down to the humblest lover of parks. By targeting the year 1966—the year the NPS would be fifty years old and a date when annual park visitation was expected to rise to unprecedented heights, an anticipated 80 million visitors—the hope was that the NPS would be, in Tilden's words, finally "adequate to the dignity of the institution, to its high place in the Nation's life, and to the recreational and cultural welfare of our people."

The plan was not without controversy, however. The NPS faced criticism from both inside and outside the agency. Agency critics were concerned about the amount of massive construction, and members of Congress were especially concerned about the cost of the program. In response, Director Wirth asked Tilden to write the text of a brochure that would educate people about the needs of the park system and advocate for implementation of MISSION 66. Tilden responded enthusiastically. For him, MISSION 66 was an opportunity

Source: Draft of manuscript by Freeman Tilden for MISSION 66 brochure on interpretation dated March 10, 1957, in National Archives and Records Administration, College Park, Maryland; Record Group 79, entry 16-A, "Records Concerning Audits and Accounts" (1933–60), box 19 (1952–53).

to make the "interpretation program more fruitful, more readily available, and more enjoyable."

In this essay, Tilden sought to accomplish two main objectives: to explain the importance of parks, and to describe what interpretation is and could be to existing and future park visitors. In doing so, he explains the relative strengths and limitations of various interpretive methods and techniques. His scenario describes the "ideal" interpretive experience.

"Why do people love to visit the parks?" It is a question that somehow reminds us of the common expression, "the average person." Really, there isn't any such person. Yet, for working purposes, we have to imagine one—a fictitious character that will represent a fair norm of desires and behavior. So, being similarly arbitrary, we can safely say that people go to the parks because of a keen realization that no picture or printed word, however brilliant, can do more than whet an appetite to experience with one's own senses the grandeur and wonder that nature has formed. No textbook, however instructive, can convey the feeling of reality that comes to us when we stand in the very places, among the identical objects, where our history has been wrought by the will and courage and ideals of the earlier days of the nation.

Even before the days of Columbus there were people living on our continent; people with hopes and aims not so greatly different from ourselves. But somehow we fail to feel kinship with them until we have visited the villages and houses where they lived and loved and worked for their livings. That is the happy and fruitful experience beside which the written word is pale.

Let us briefly glimpse what of America's story is comprised within this National Park System. So far as nature has provided us with beauty, and with the titanic examples of her forces, and so far as we have been able to preserve in time the virginal wilderness picture that greeted the eyes of our ancestors when they moved westward on their conquering march, our primeval parks represent superlative examples of many types. Beauty is everywhere, and we can see nature's handiwork without going far from our homes. But these are wilderness places of such consummate quality that they are world famous. And since they *are* wilderness, and because man must for his best mental and spiritual health retain the possibility of access to such unexploited retreats, they become every year more vital to the national welfare as with every passing year we become more urbanized.

The other side of the National Park System deals with our national history, including the lives of the aboriginal peoples. In this great chain of shrines—from the struggle of England, France, and Spain for supremacy, through our westward expansion and our great Domestic War, down to more recent years of invention and progress—the growth of the country becomes for visitors a living reality. It is the past brought into the pulsating present.

When you visit one of the great primeval parks for the first time, the impact of so much grandeur and beauty is overwhelming. At first you feel dwarfed, insignificant, even humbled, in spite of the eager intake of the perfection of the scene. But if your experience parallels that of most of us, these feelings are succeeded by a queer sort of exultation that all this loveliness and wonder is not foreign, not apart, but that you share something with it as it shares something with you.

From that moment your curiosity is stimulated. What does it all mean? How came it as it is? What were these giant forces that created the picture before you, and what is its history? For the natural scene has a history just as much as the battleground of Manassas or Independence Hall. You wish to know. You wish to understand. You desire to take home with you something more than the picture in the mind's eye, unforgettable as that may be. Where can you ask the questions you would like to ask; where can you learn the things you want to know—not later, but now—in the full freshness of the adventure?

To serve you, in this most vital and enduring part of your park experience, is the service we call *interpretation*.

It is not otherwise in the historical areas of the National Park System. In these, perhaps you come with a rather greater anticipation of what you are likely to see. Yet the first thrill, within one of these shrines, is merely to be there, to be in contact with the thing itself rather than at second hand; to tread the very soil where great actions have taken place, or where great men have lived and labored and died. But again, after this first feeling passes, you wish to know the story of it; not merely the incidents of local import, but how such events affected the flow of your nation's history, and therefore how it affected your own life and lot. You have many questions. You are quickened in the impulse to comprehend the larger significance.

And again, this is the clear duty of the National Park Service: not merely to preserve the piece of hallowed ground, but to make it full of meaning to the visitor. This is *interpretation*. In the very place, surrounded by the very memorials, you enjoy by understanding. From that fuller understanding follows a sense of personal custody. "This is my legacy. I must protect it." Thus interpretation becomes also an instrument of the safekeeping of our parks.

It is not necessary to define the word "interpretation" here. What has already been said, plus the following description of the many forms of interpretive work, will make clear enough the purpose of this visitor service. That will be better than any stark definition.

It is obvious that there can be no such thing as interpretation unless someone, somewhere, has by diligence and professional skill ascertained a body of facts. Hearsay, legend, and guess will not do. The work of eliciting the highlights, and telling them in that necessarily brief form demanded by the limited time the visitor can be expected to devote to such an end, is the work of the interpreter, who must know the essence and depth of his subject and reveal it without cluttering it with the less important details. But he depends wholly upon the naturalist, the historian, and the archaeologist for that scrupulously accurate factual knowledge that is his to interpret.

Consider, a moment, the gamut of natural and human history that is comprised in the National Park System! There is scarcely a phenomenon of nature's work that is not represented in one or more of the scenic and scientific preserves. The face of our land discloses the evidence of all the colossal forces that have built and torn it down, rebuilt and again torn down, in order to produce the spectacular and aesthetic scenery seen by the park visitor. There is much, however, that is to be observed and studied only by the specialist, whose finds make it possible to piece together what we see and what we cannot see, and reconstruct the earth-story of 2 billion years.

These specialists are skilled and devoted men and women, and generally speaking the need for continuing research is as great as ever. Where there is doubt as to the explanation of a certain wonder, the geologist and the archaeologist may team up together and give the answer, as was the case at Crater Lake. It is now possible to say to the visitor who asks how that deep blue lake came to be as it is— and what thoughtful visitor has failed to ask?—that he is seeing a volcanic mountain that lost so much of its interior contents that it collapsed.

The historian and the archaeologist joined forces to reveal long-buried evidences of early settlements of the colonists that came to conquer the New World. Who of us that visited Jamestown, in former years, ever had more than a vague notion of what our first English settlement really looked like when its first inhabitants were clinging desperately to the fringe of a wilderness and trying to adapt them-selves to the rigors of a strange environment? In preparation for the observance of the 350th anniversary of this Virginia settlement in 1957, the utmost resources of the specialist were called upon. As a result, there is a Jamestown that we do not merely visit, or *look at*, but a Jamestown that we can *live*. It is no longer just a name and a loca-tion—we can think of it with the reflection: "I, myself, if I had been living then, would have shared this sort of life." And that, after all, is one of the aims of true interpretation—to bring any instances of the historic past so vividly to observers that they feel a part of it.

Of course, researchers contribute more than ammunition for in-terpretation, for they are constantly called upon to supply informa-tion vital to park management. But so far as the public is directly concerned, the interpreter is the person who tells the visitor what he wants to know.

It frequently happens that the specialist is also the person who comes in direct contact with the visitor, just as it happens that the ranger, whose primary function is the protection of the park, spends much time helping the visitor. Here, the naturalist, the historian, the archaeologist must play two very different roles. The interpreter's aim with the general visitor looking for interpretation is to be as informal and nontechnical as possible, dwelling on the spirit of the area rather than its letter, but also speak with authority. Interpreters must also be prepared to deal with the expert and the student, who have come not so much for holiday as to find, or check upon, concrete details.

Remember, too, that these park areas are also priceless founts for the experts and the students who are continually pursuing their professional studies within them. You may well call them outdoor laboratories, or classrooms. Through such special-purpose visitors the torch of accurate knowledge is carried forth into many outside organizations, where it, too, becomes the basis for more interpretation, perhaps in the form of reading matter, perhaps by oral communication.

What, then, does this program of greatly improved interpretation mean to *you*, the prospective visitor to the national parks?

It can best be realized if you will imagine yourself visiting a national park with your family. The flood of Americans into our parks comes during the summer months, for that is when the schools are out. Ideally, it would be fine if more people could arrange to enjoy the areas at a time when the weather conditions are just as good, or even better, and when the crowds have diminished. But we have to face the facts as they exist.

So you and your family have arrived at one of the national parks. If you happen to be visiting a park for the first time, would it not be a wonderful saving in time and energy if there were a place you could go at once to get acquainted with all that the place has to offer you? Courteous and helpful as the uniformed ranger at the checking station may be, it is manifestly impossible for this individual to tell you all that you would wish to know.

In the lean years of the National Park Service, many a visitor has justly felt a sense of frustration in driving about aimlessly in search of "a place to start." MISSION 66 plans to remedy that lack. By the end of its anniversary year the service will have more than a hundred "visitor centers" to which you and your family can go immediately. The largest parks will have more than one such facility.

Here in such a visitor center you find a building designed for exactly this orientation purpose, not a make-do. With the aid of all the devices of information and interpretation that skill and ingenuity have created, and with the advice and help of a trained personnel, you will know how you can make your visit yield the greatest enjoyment in the time you have to spend—which with most of us is sadly too brief. There will be, where the need exists, accommodations for giving special talks for school groups. Museum exhibits, dioramas, relief models, a library fitted either for browsing or for research, will bring at once to visitors the distinct qualities of the park, making clear not only *what* and *why*, but also its significance in the whole collection of our national treasure. Here, at the outset, in no cold or labored way, the visitor will understand his own personal obligation to protect and properly use this—and all—national preserves.

Each one of the new visitor centers is precisely adapted to the needs of its particular area. Let us consider just one of these centers, as an example. Dinosaur National Monument, in Utah and Colorado, is famous as the richest deposit of dinosaur fossil remains in the country. Of course, this monument is far more than a reptilian boneyard. It happens also to include some of our finest scenery and some of our most spectacular canyons. It is not often that the layman ever has a chance to see the bones of this "terrible lizard" in the very place where he gave up his life many millions of years ago. Indeed, only those who can visit certain large museums ever have a real sense of the existence of these creatures. Besides affording that "place to start," already mentioned, the visitor center at Dinosaur Monument headquarters gives an "in-place" display that will never be forgotten by those who go there. The building's back wall will look directly upon those fossilized remains, reliefed in the encompassing rock. What a place for interpretation to begin! Can you imagine any illustrations or book descriptions that could so bring you at elbow with a period of the earth's history when part of our native land swarmed with fantastic reptiles of enormous size—one of them eighty-four feet long, but with a brain that hardly matched its bulk. Out of the haze of evolution they came; strangely they disappeared; but your children can go back to school and say that they now *really understand*.

At the visitor center you and your family will find at once how and when you can participate in a conducted trip led by a trained naturalist or historian or archaeologist. Much thought has gone into the adequate training of this interpretive personnel. Dealing with you, and the rest of the public, is a skill in itself. You want information and explanation, but you want it in words that you can readily comprehend. You are not a specialist, and you do not expect to be. Some of the names of rocks, of trees and flowers, some of the historical events, you have learned about in your school years, but in the pressure of business and professional life, the memories are vague. A renewal of appreciation of these half-forgotten things is like clasping the hand of an old friend.

Whether the conducted trip is done afoot or whether by using your car you take part in a caravan tour, the greatest pleasure and stimulation will come to you if the group is not too large. From lack of personnel the National Park Service has often been obliged to perform this duty with overcrowded groups. The very essence of the conducted trip depends upon your feeling of intimacy with the guide who is giving you the story, and upon your ability to be reasonably close to him. The hearty acceptance of the MISSION 66 plans is an assurance of greater enjoyment, in the coming years, for those who go upon conducted trips.

But you and your family may be among those who, without shunning other folks as a principle, yet would rather at times be entirely upon your own—to amble at your own pace, spend as much time as you please upon the objects of your interest.

For you, then, are the many self-guiding walks, both in the wild places and in the parks devoted to history and prehistory. The idea of placing labels along a trail, indicating the names and natures of plants, rock formations or other features, or having numbered stakes that correspond with the items of an explanatory leaflet made available at the start of the trip, not only is in itself an admirable interpretive medium, but was for some years a device forced upon the National Park Service by lack of adequate personnel. The self-guiding trails delight many visitors and are so valuable a form of interpretation that they deserve to be greatly expanded.

An especial merit of these trails is that most of them are not beyond the walking ability of those who are unfitted for more strenuous effort. The needs of older and less active people are always in the mind of our interpreters, since these folks commonly bring a maturity that makes their adventure more personal and meaningful. Nor are the children forgotten. Far from it. Wherever conditions warrant it, there are provisions for school groups. Teachers realize keenly the importance of this contact with original objects and with the actual scene where our history has been made. And the National Park Service never forgets its younger visitors, brought thus early to a recognition of the significance of what the parks represent, are the future protectors of these national resources.

Probably the high point of enjoyment and stimulation—the memory taken back home and treasured by most visitors to the "wilderness" parks—is the campfire program. You and your family may already know this experience. There is nothing quite like it in all the world. Not only is it typical of the very spirit in which the National Park System was conceived: it is America itself. Picture again the scene: here are people gathered together from every state in the Union, fresh from a day in which they have looked upon exceptional beauties and natural marvels, pleasantly tired but still in the mood for one last event before they go to their beds.

Now, with the leaping flames reflecting a rosy glow against the surrounding trees, is the moment when such a group can catch something of the feeling that inspired the free-roving explorers and adventurers of the pioneer day of their country. The fur trappers sat around such a blaze at their rendezvous; the Montana men who first told the world that the wonders of Yellowstone were indeed no fictions but wholly true—*they* discussed a future people-owned park as they gathered around just such a campfire. The spiritual quality of contact with the wild is borne in upon us in this fire-lighted darkness, even though we are not conscious of it at the moment.

This is the time, in such a gathering, that the interpreter can truly project the meaning of the natural world; the community of living things—bird, animal, insect, flower, and tree—and their part in our own human existence. There is group singing, and if somebody is off-key, no matter. The feeling of real fellowship is the important matter. Then comes a talk by the interpreter, sometimes illustrated on the screen. It may be about the geology of the region; it may be about the animals who are not, at the very moment, too far distant from the fire; perhaps it deals with the Mountain Men who first invaded this wilderness—whatever the subject, the aim is to link what one has seen with the larger truths of nature and history that give meaning to our own life. This is a chance, too, to tell what the parks mean as preserved natural resources of the nation. What better moment could there be to invoke the strong desire of the visitor to keep them inviolate, and to use them with loving care?

If these campfire programs have sometimes failed to achieve their full educational and inspirational end, the reason has often been that competent interpreters have been lacking, and that proper facilities have not been provided. Not that huge amphitheaters are desirable. Quite the contrary. The circles should be as small in size as is practicable. In some cases the rudest possible conditions, as to physical equipment, will suffice; though the audiovisual devices must be the best obtainable. As to just what constitutes the ideal-size gathering, there is room for many opinions. The one thing sure is that every visitor should be provided, some way, with this classic campfire experience. It is a precious link with nature and the American story.

The excellence of the National Park System museums is world famous. They are an essential interpretive service in every area. They do not compete with the larger Museum, which is the *place itself*. They do for the visitor what he cannot possibly hope to do for himself; they show him the component parts of the whole. His eyes and his time are limitations. The leaf in the sandstone, telling the tale of millions of years of geologic time, is there. But you and your family would never be likely to find it. Some naturalist has discovered it and placed it in the museum. Those sedimentary rocks, layer upon layer, in Grand Canyon, are a delight to the outward eye. But the inward eye needs help to understand the meaning they hold. The battlefield memorial park may be in physical aspect pretty much as it was when warring men passed over it nearly a hundred years ago, but when you look at the diorama, executed with the skill and art of the experts of the National Park Service laboratory staff, you are brought to a sharp realization that this was what your great-grandfather may have seen; what he may have endured.

You and your family see the geysers of Yellowstone; you see where Mount Lassen's outburst sent a river of mud down its flank, sweeping forests before it; you see the homes of the cliff dwellers and the strange salt flats of Death Valley. Seeing them, you want to know the answers while you are upon the ground; and the museum, simply and understandably, related the parts to the whole. In these museums are safely stored the irreplaceable objects that cannot be handled, but must be viewed if you are to understand the essence of the place. Whether you and your family will want to start with the museum and go from there to the Museum—the park itself—or the other way about, is for you to decide. But it is certain that a visit to one, without reference to the other, would result in an incomplete realization of the significance of the shrine.

Of great importance in the interpretation scheme are the roadside markers and exhibits. Indeed, they may be called the basic implements, for it is unfortunately true that some hurried travelers in the parks obtain most of their understanding from these. Consequently the "interpretive" sign, as distinguished from what is merely directional or informational, must be brief, must be enlivening, must be much in little. A marker can be, and often is, both informational and interpretive. The aim of the National Park Service is toward an improvement of all such highway "literature" and the creation of such well-placed turnouts, overlooks, and other facilities that will realize their best use.

The new highway on the east side of Jackson Hole, in Wyoming's Grand Teton National Park, supplies a good example of the effectiveness of the wayside exhibit and the interpretive sign. Though a full appreciation of the manifold beauties and geologic story of the region requires a visit to the museums, or to the written word, it is still possible by using the strategic overlooks that face the great Alpine range to get a fair comprehension of what nature has done here and how slow time, acting with many tools, has sculptured the rugged landscape.

Within the Division of Interpretation is included a busy and invaluable service known as the Branch of Information. The line between information and interpretation, despite the fact that they are essentially two different things, is a shadowy one. The enormous quantities of free folders sent from the Washington office, or supplies in every area of the system, are interpretive as well as informational.

In addition to the free folders, a demand has grown for something, sold at a low price, that will take the reader farther into the story of the natural and historical parks. This demand has been met by the production of a series of authoritative "handbooks." So successful have these publications proved that the revenues from them, accruing to the United States Treasury, have exceeded the costs of printing.

The criterion for all publications of the National Park Service is, first, that they shall be as accurate as the highest professional knowledge can insure. They must be written in such language, and employing such terms, as will be understood by a person of common-school education. They are intended to answer all the questions that would normally be asked about any of the preserved areas. But above all, the aim is to picture "relationships"—between nature and man, between man and fellow man. To know the name of a flower, or the kind of tree one sees, is good; but they are facts that tend to slip away. To understand that plants and animals are members of a community, interdependent and "trading" with each other, no less than you and your family are members of a close-knit neighborhood—this is the truth that abides in the mind. To project such ultimate and vital truths, illustrated by what one can observe in our national parks, is the aim of our interpretation.

Finally, as valuable aids to good interpretation, we turn to the devices know as "audiovisual." The National Park Service came slowly and with much thought to the use of these aids. Nobody dreams that they can ever take the place of the warm personal contact with a human being, into whose eyes you can look when you talk. But the service looked longingly toward these devices to plug that alarming gap between the mushrooming visitation and the inadequate personnel that could provide the needed interpretive services. It is a fact, too, that certain audiovisual devices fit themselves better into a specific purpose than a man can do.

For some years, however, the audiovisual mechanisms had what the technicians call "bugs." They were just not good enough nor reliable enough. That has changed. Experimentation in the laboratory of the National Park Service, as well as the production of highly efficient devices by the manufacturers, makes it certain that we shall have more and more of these helps as the years come. At the very moment when this is being written, slide projectors, tape recorders, and other aids are being sent out to the parks. Some of them can be operated by the visitor himself. They are, in fact, no longer a makeshift to take the place of uniformed rangers who were not there because of lack of funds. They are interpreters in their own right. You and your family will enjoy what they can do for you.

These are the interpretive services offered to you in the national parks. They are yours to accept; yours to decline. Do many visitors make use of them? Abundantly, they do. But figures do not tell the story of fulfilled desires, of satisfied thirst for knowledge, or of spiritual uplift; but so far as figures count, conducted trips are enjoyed by millions of visitors each year.

More impressive than numerals is the sight—so frequently observed—of a man carrying a small sleeping infant in his arms along a fairly rugged trail, just because he cannot bear to miss the chance of learning from nature's own handwriting, interpreted by a naturalist of enthusiasm and solid scholarship. Only in such an instance do you come to know what this experience means to so many of our people.

INDEX

119–25, 152–57; love of, 130–31, 149; in mindsight, 161; mystery of, 119–25, 150; of nature, 119–21, 148–54, 188–89; as surprise, 119–20; threats to, 148–49

Being vs. not-being, 174, 178

Bennett-Arcane party, 108

Bible, 57, 68

Big Bend National Park: beauty of, 124; demonstrations in, 106; parts vs. wholes of, 69–70

Blindness, 166–69, 171

Blue Ridge Parkway: demonstrations at, 103; inscriptions on, 95–96

Boggs, Samuel Whittemore, 72–73

Bosanquet, Bernard, 119

Boston Globe, 3

Boston Herald, 3

Bowman, Isaiah, 62

Brevity in inscriptions, 95–97

Brookgreen Gardens: beauty of, 120–21; inscriptions at, 94

Bryant, Harold C., vii, 62, 162

Bumpus, Hermon Carey, 27, 62, 63, 162

Burnet, John, 68

Busyness, 118

Cacti, 106

Campbell, Thomas, 113

Campfire programs, 123 (ill.); gadgets in, 137; role of, 20, 171, 195–96; size of, 196

Camping, 101

C&O Canal, 107

Cannons, 83, 105

Canyon de Chelly National Monument: animation at, 111; provocation at, 64–65

Capitalization, 95–96

Carcassonne, 126

Carlsbad Caverns, 39 (ill.)

Carlyle, Thomas, 130, 131

Carriage rides, 107–8

Castillo de San Marcos National Monument: children's programs at, 83; constructive inaction at, 180; demonstrations at, 105; participation at, 105; Tilden's programs at, 9; understanding of people at, 128–30

Cave paintings, 154

Chaco Culture National Historic Park, 32 (ill.)

Chamfort, Nicholas, 37

Champlain, Samuel de, 138

Charleston News and Courier, 3

Chesterton, G. K., 55

Children: accessibility for, 194; approach to interpreting for, 18, 35, 76–85; as focus of programs, 14, 78 (ill.); language used with, 76–77, 79; previsit material for, 83–85; senses used by, 79–81, 80 (ill.), 84 (ill.); writing for, 82

"Christmas Message, A" (Fosdick), 26

Civil War sites, 40 (ill.); amateurs at, 141; beauty of, 156; information at, 50–51; inscriptions at, 92; parts vs. wholes of, 70–72; recreating past at, 102–3. *See also* specific sites

Clemens, Samuel, 48

Cliff dwellings, 108

Coins, 142

Coleridge, Samuel Taylor, 127

Colonial Williamsburg. *See* Williamsburg, Colonial

Communication: interpretation as form of, 1–2

Composition, 92, 95–98

Conduct, beauty of, 155–56

Congress, U.S., 187

"Constructive Aspect of Inaction, The" (Tilden), 20–21, 174–81

Continuity, 128

Cook County Forest Preserve District: children's programs in, 76, 81; inscriptions in, 94–95

Cooperstown: children's programs at, 76, 81; demonstrations at, 105; excess in, 116; Tilden's visit to, 9

Corbett, John, 42

Cranes, whooping, 144

Crater Lake National Park: accessibility of, 166–69; research at, 27, 191

Craters of the Moon National Monument, 121

Cruise of the Beagle, The (Darwin), 45–47

"Culture" (Emerson), 99

Cumberland Falls, 181

Custis, George Washington Parke, 111

Custis, Mary, 111

Custis-Lee Mansion: animation at, 9, 109–11; research at, 30; Tilden's visits to, 9

Cuthbert Lake Rookery, 164

Dabney, Walt, vii, 12, 17

Darwin, Charles, 45–47, 124, 161, 165

Death Valley National Monument: inscriptions at, 90–92, 93, 96; participation at, 108; research at, 30

Demonstrations, 103–6, 104 (ill.)

Desert Museum, 105–6

Deserts: demonstrations on, 105–6; inscriptions in, 99–100

De Soto, Hernando, 48

Dickens, Charles, 170

Diffusion of interest, 116–18

Dinosaur National Monument: research at, 30; visitor center at, 193

Diotima, 131–32

Direct contact, 133, 134, 136 (ill.)

Dodge, Natt, 106

Doing vs. not-doing, 174, 178

Drury, Newton, 6, 7

"Each and All" (Emerson), 185

Ecology: in children's programs, 76–77; definition of, 77; improvements to teaching of, 17; use of term, 14

Education: adult, 13–14, 17, 145; and beauty, 152–53, 157; environmental, 13–14, 17; imagination in, 53–54; interpretation as, 17, 18, 54, 60, 152–53; origins of in NPS programs, 60–64; as science vs. art, 53

Educational Advisory Board, 62

Emerson, Ralph Waldo: on archaeology, 72; on beauty, 148, 156; on children, 76, 82; on grand tours, 161; humor of, 99, 183; influence on Tilden, 174; on nature-human relations, 65–67, 119; on provocation, 18, 60; on relating experiences, 36, 43; Thoreau and, 182–86; on whole man, 75

Entertainment, 162–63

Enthusiasm in writing, 93

Environmental crisis, 13–14, 17

Epigraphy. *See* Inscription

European grand tours, 161–62

Everglades National Park, 163–64

Excess, 112–18

Experiences of visitors, 18, 34, 36–43

Expert visitors, 191–92

"Fable" (Emerson), 185

Facts. *See* Information

Falling Leaf Lodge, 162

Farmers' Museum: children's programs at, 81; demonstrations at, 105; Tilden's visit to, 9

Feiss, Carl, 128

Fiction, 3, 6

Fifth Essence, The (Tilden), 8

Fitness: as element in beauty, 121

Folders, free, 197

Fort Frederica National Monument: research at, 30–33

Fort Laramie National Historic Site: amateurs at, 140–41

Fort Necessity National Battlefield: research at, 30

Fosdick, Harry Emerson, 26

Francis of Assisi, Saint, 94

Franconia Notch, 98

Franklin, Benjamin, 145–47

Fratricide, 70

Freeman Tilden Award, 2

Fund-raising, 7–8, 9

Gadgetry, 133–37, 198

Gardening, 183

Gassendi, Pierre, 101

Geological and paleontological sites: amateurs at, 141–42; children's programs at, 82–83; information at, 46–48; inscriptions at, 90–92, 98; participation at, 108–9; visitor centers at, 193. *See also* specific sites

Gettysburg Address, 57

Glaciation, 49

Goethe, Charles M., 62, 161–62

Goethe, Johann Wolfgang von, 148

Goethe, Mrs. Charles M., 62

Goode, Brown, 38

Grand Canyon National Park, 29 (ill.), 181, 196; constructive inaction in, 181; observation stations at, 172

Grand Teton National Park: constructive inaction at, 180; love of, 130–31; markers in, 10, 197

Grant, Ulysses S., 70, 156, 180–81

Greece, ancient: coins of, 142; inscriptions of, 89–90; leisure in, 139; philosophy of, 131–32

Greenbush Creek, 141–42

Greenfield Village: children's programs at, 76, 83

Griggs, Robert F., 47

Hall, Ansel F., 60, 162

Handbooks, 197

Happiness: of amateurs, 138–47; interpreters as middlemen of, 37

origins of, 16, 161–63; philosophy underlying, 8–9, 10, 26, 174–81; use of term, 10–11, 25–26. *See also* Principles

Interpreters: age of, 83; connecting with visitors, 38; definitions of interpretation for, 33–34; happy amateurs created by, 140–47; humility of, 74; love of people by, 126–30; love of subject by, 130–31; as middlemen of beauty, 152; as middlemen of happiness, 37; vs. nature writers, 182; philosophy of, 164–65; as poets, 54–55; relationship with visitors, 36; researchers as, 48, 191; self-knowledge of, 54–55; summary of job of, 164–65; teachers as, 26–27, 164–65

Interpreting Our Heritage (Tilden): distribution of, 11; editions of, 11, 20; influence of, vii, 1–2, 16–19; publication of, vii, 11; reception of, 10–11; writing of, 9–11

"Interpretive Ideal, An" (Tilden), 17, 20, 21, 187–99

Interpretive writing. *See* Writing

Ironworks demonstrations, 105

Irwin, Wallace, 45

Irwin, Will, 45

Jackson, William Henry, 181

James, Henry, 126

James, William, 156

Jamestown, research at, 30, 191

Jefferson, Thomas, 110 (ill.)

Johnson, Lady Bird, 155

Johnson, Lyndon Baines, 148, 149

Johnson, Samuel, 138

Jones, Louis C., 81

Journalism, Tilden's work in, 2–3

Jowett, Benjamin, 131

Kant, Immanuel, 119, 149

Katmai, Mount, 47

Kellogg, Vernon, 62, 162

King René's Daughter (Hertz), 167

Klingle Mansion, 82

Knopf, Alfred, 7

Kosciusko, Thaddeus, 113

Labels: in museums, 38–41; on self-guiding walks, 194

Ladies' Home Journal, 3

Lafayette Square, 113

Landor, Walter Savage, 24

Language: in children's programs, 76–77, 79; evolution of, 138; excess in, 113–14; in inscriptions, 90–92, 96; in storytelling, 58; technical, 41, 43; telegraphic, 96; written vs. oral, 47

Laura Spelman Rockefeller Memorial Fund, 62, 162

Lechuguilla plants, 106

Lee, Robert E., 41–42, 156, 180–81

Lee, Ronald, 9, 10, 11, 96, 111, 120

Leisure, 138–39, 145

Lexington Green, 93–94

Liberty Bell, 1, 66 (ill.)

Life on the Mississippi (Twain), 48

Lightness in writing, 99–100

Lincoln, Abraham, 57, 151, 156

Little Tour in France, A (James), 126

Living history: vs. animation, 9; demonstrations in, 104 (ill.)

Living Past, The (Merriam), 111

Lizards, 177–78

Love, 126–32; of beauty, 130–31, 149; in humor, 98; of people, 126–30; as principle of interpretation, 19, 35, 132; of subject, 130–31; and understanding, 67, 128–30; in writing process, 93, 95

Mabry's Mill, 103
Making of Citizens, The (Merriam), 37
Mann, Bob, 94–95, 98
Manos, 109
"Man the Reformer" (Emerson), 183
Manual labor, 183
Manucy, Albert, 83
Marcus Aurelius, 119
Markers: made by Tilden, 10; master, 93; roadside, 197. *See also* Inscription(s)
Martin, Mabel S. *See* Tilden, Mabel
Master-marker, 93
Mather, Cotton, 107
Mather, Stephen T., 60–62, 63, 162
Mather Training Center, 2, 15 (ill.), 19, 174
Mattes, Merrill, 56
McLean House, 180–81
McLoughlin, John, 102
Mellon, Paul, 9
Mencken, H. L., 3
Merriam, C. E., 37
Merriam, John: on art vs. science, 53, 54; on Canyon de Chelly, 64–65, 111; on demonstrations, 103; on education, 62, 63; *The Living Past*, 111; in origins of interpretation, 162; on visitor interests, 38
Mesa Verde National Park, 62
Metalsmiths, 124

Metaphors, 56, 57, 183
Metates, 109
Michelson, Albert, 53
Mill demonstrations, 103
Miller, Lloye, 162
Mills, Enos, 16
Mind, beauty of, 152–54
Mindsight, 20, 161–65
Minerals, amateur study of, 144–45
MISSION 66 initiative, 7–8, 9, 187–88, 192, 194
Mississippi River, 48
Missouri: in Civil War, 70
Mithridatic wars, 139
Montana, highway signs in, 98–99
Montcalm, General, 99
Montezuma Castle: inscriptions at, 96; participation at, 108
Monticello, 110 (ill.)
Mood, 120, 121
Morals, 14, 156
Mount Rainier National Park, 169, 171
Movement in inscriptions, 97–98
Muir, John, 16
Mulliken, Robert S., 153
Murie, Olaus, 180
Museum Is a Story, A (film), 83
Museums: beauty in, 120–21, 124; children's programs at, 79, 83; demonstrations at, 105–6; excess in, 113, 114–16; gadgets in, 134, 136 (ill.); inscriptions in, 92, 94; observation stations as, 172; parts vs. wholes in, 196; relating to visitors at, 38–41, 196; resistance to, 173; role of, 171–73, 196
Music, 109–11

Order of nature, beauty of, 152–54
Oregon Trail, 108, 111
Overlooks, 119–20

Packard, Fred M., 11
Paintings, 113
Paleontological sites. *See* Geological and paleontological sites
Parker, Harry C., 56
Parker, John, 93
Parks. *See* National parks; State parks; specific parks
Participation, 71 (ill.), 106–9; and animation, 111; through camping, 101; definition of, 106–7; demonstration turned into, 105; at historic sites, 105, 106–9
Parts vs. wholes, 18, 35, 52, 68–75, 196
Pascal, Blaise, 112
Pemberton, John C., 70–72
People, love of, 126–30
Peopling of historic sites, 102–3, 111
Pereskius, 142
Personalities of visitors, 18, 34, 36–43
Personnel shortages, 192, 194, 198
Pest control, 177–78
Petrified Forest National Park, 170
Philosophy: Greek, 131–32; of interpreters, 165; underlying interpretation, 8–9, 10, 26
Physical participation, 107
Physis, 131
Piano music, 109–11
Pictures in inscriptions, 98
Pinkley, Frank, 130, 131
Pioneers, 101, 106, 108, 195

Pipes, 108, 154
Pipestone National Monument, 108
Plants: in demonstrations, 105–6; gardening of, 183
Plato, 149, 174, 178
Plotinus, 119
Poetry, 54–55, 185
Pollution, 149
Prehistoric sites, 101–11; amateurs at, 141–42; beauty of, 154; importance of, 188, 189; participation in, 108–9; parts vs. wholes of, 72; reasons for visiting, 188; recreating past at, 102; relating to visitors at, 38–41, 42. *See also* specific sites
Presentations, 174
Preservation: of beauty, 148–49, 151; as goal, 140; inaction in, 178–81; interpretation leading to, 65. *See also* Protection
Previsit material, 83–85
Primitive sites. *See* Natural areas
Principles of interpretation, 25–35; additional, 19–21, 34; application of, 10; definitions of interpretation and, 17, 25, 33–34; development of, 10; influence of, vii, 18; list of six, 18, 34–35; and mindsight, 164–65; need for, 26; principle one, 18, 34, 36–43; principle two, 18, 34, 44–52; principle three, 18, 35, 53–58; principle four, 18, 35, 59–67; principle five, 18, 35, 68–75; principle six, 18, 35, 76–85
Protection: as goal, 140; interpreta-

tion leading to, 8, 65, 190; need for, 148–49, 151

Provocation, interpretation as, 18, 35, 59–67, 161, 165

Publications, NPS, 197–98

Public relations, 6, 7

Quebec, inscriptions in, 99

Questions: from adults, 74, 83; from children, 83; in writing process, 92–93

Quotations in inscriptions, 93–95

Rangers, role of, 191, 192

Rats, 177

Relationships: between nature and humans, 65–67, 119; in NPS publications, 198; between visitors and interpreters, 36

Relics, 92

Relief maps, 166, 168

Research: for children's programs, 82; importance of, 27–33, 31 (ill.), 190–91; information derived from, 48–49

Research and Education in the National Parks (Bryant and Atwood), 62, 63

Researchers: as interpreters, 48, 191; role of, 190–91

Revelation: interpretation as, 26–27; of order of nature, 152–54

Rhetoric, 58. *See also* Language

Roadside signs, 98–99, 197

Rock Creek Park: children's programs at, 82–83; demonstrations in, 103

Rockefeller, John D., Jr., 107–8, 120

Rocks, amateur study of, 144–45

Rome, ancient, 139, 142

Roosevelt, Franklin Delano, 41, 102

Royce, Josiah, 149

Ruskin, John, 69, 121

Russell, Carl P., 62

Saguaro cactus, 106

St. Patrick's Day, 111

St. Paul's Cathedral, 90

San Francisco earthquake, 45

Sarráchaca, Pedro, 53

Saturday Evening Post, 3

Science: amateur study of, 142–47; beauty in, 153; in inscriptions, 90–92; interpretation as, 53; interpretation of, 46–47, 48

Scott, Sir Walter, 44

Sculpture, 94, 120–21

Self-guided interpretation, 121, 171, 194

Selfishness, 37

Self-knowledge, 54–55

Senses: beauty apprehended by, 149–50, 152; of blind people, 166–69, 171; in children's programs, 79–81

Sheep, 30

Shellbach, Louis, vii

Shorey, Paul, 149

Short stories, 3

Sight: beauty apprehended through, 149, 152; in blindness, 166–69, 171; in children, 83; limits of, 164, 165, 167, 169

Signs. *See* Inscription(s)

Simonides, 89–90

Sinnott Memorial Observation Station, 166

Smell, 81

Smith, "White Mountains," 130–31

Smithy, 124

Snails, 175, 177

Socrates, 124, 131–32

Soul of things, 27, 67

Sovulewski, Gabriel, 130, 131

Specialists, role of, 190–91

Spring Mill State Park, 103

Squirrels, 175–77

Standard (newspaper), 3

State parks, 12. *See also* specific parks

State Parks, The (Tilden), 12

Steel Institute, 105

Storytelling: art of, 55–58; to children, 83; in classical inscriptions, 89–90; in museums, 173

Students. *See* Children; Education

Style, 35

Superlatives, 79, 114

Surprise, beauty as, 119–20

Switzerland, 161–62

Tahoe, Lake, 62, 162

Taste, 81

Teacher(s): as interpreters, 26–27; nature as, 166–73

Telegraphic writing, 96

Telescopes, 118, 172

Thackeray, William Makepeace, 98

"That Elderly Schoolma'am: Nature" (Tilden), 7, 20, 166–73

Thinking in writing process, 92–95

Thompson, J. Arthur, 144

Thoreau, Henry David, 21, 161, 182–86

Tilden, Freeman: career of, 2–7; death of, 2, 14–16; on environmental education, 13–14; family of, 3; life of, 2–7; other writings on interpretation, 19–21; photos of, xii, 4, 5, 146; writing *Interpreting Our Heritage*, 9–11, 16–19; writings on national parks, 7–9, 12–16, 19. *See also* specific writings

Tilden, Mabel, 3, 5 (ill.)

Tilden, Samuel, 2

Toads, 177–78

Tonto National Monument, 72

Touch, 79–81, 82, 168

Trails, self-guiding, 171, 194

Treasury, U.S., 197

Trees, petrified, 170

Trends (bulletin), 19

Truth, 33, 67

Twain, Mark, 48

"Two Concord Men in a Boat" (Tilden), 21, 182–86

Ugliness, 150, 151, 155

Understanding, 65–67; love and, 67, 128–30; as mission of interpretation, 190; of people, 127–30

Ure Pass, inscriptions in, 98

Uspallata Range, 46–47

Utility, 148, 151

Valley Forge National Military Park, 51 (ill.)

Vandalism, 81, 103

Vanderbilt, Frederick, 102

Van Dyke, Henry, 64

Vantage points, 120

Vicksburg National Military Park: parts vs. wholes of, 70–72

Vietnam War, 156